DECORATIVE PAINTING

PAINTING ROSES *WITH* DEANNE FORTNAM MDA

NORTH LIGHT BOOKS
CINCINNATI, OHIO

DEDICATION

For Douglas, your unconditional love, friendship and support has given me the courage to pursue my dreams. This book is also dedicated to all my wonderful painting students and friends throughout the world whose vision and confidence in my teaching keep me on a lifetime quest to learn more.

ACKNOWLEDGMENTS

Many thanks to Ron and Maria Soifert at the Covered Bridge Crafts for your generosity and support, but most especially for your friendship. Thanks also to Rosemary Reynolds of DecoArt for your generous help whenever I ask, and to Kathy Kipp of North Light for your patience with me and for having the faith that I would actually get this done. I also want to thank Anne Hevener for your most gracious hospitality. You have gone above and beyond the call of duty, and it is truly appreciated!

Other fine North Light Books are available from your local bookstore or direct from the publisher.

02 01 00 99 98   5 4 3 2 1

Library of Congress Cataloging-in-Publication Data

Fortnam, Deanne
    Painting roses with Deanne Fortnam, MDA / Deanne Fortnam.—1st ed.
       p.   cm.
    Includes index.
    ISBN 0-89134-793-3 (pbk)
    1. Roses in art.   2. Painting—Technique.   I. Title.
ND1400.F65   1998
758'.42—dc21   97-35460
                             CIP

Edited by Kathy Kipp and Jennifer Long
Production edited by Michelle Howry
Designed by Brian Roeth
Cover photo by Pamela Monfort Braun/Bronze Photography

Deanne Fortnam began decorative painting in 1982, when a friend talked her into taking a "tole" painting class: It was love at first sight the first time she side loaded a brush.

Interested in the arts since childhood, Deanne began taking drawing classes with a local artist, working primarily in charcoal and pastels until the early 1980s, when she developed an interest in decorative painting. She joined the Society of Decorative Painters in 1983, and was awarded their prestigious Master Decorative Artist certification in 1991.

Deanne currently works in many different styles in oils, acrylics and watercolors. She is a popular seminar instructor, known especially for her techniques in acrylic realism. She teaches throughout the U.S. and internationally. Deanne is widely published in the decorative painting field, including two instructional books titled *A Symphony of Classics* and *A Symphony of Classics, Volume 2*.

A native of New England, Deanne still lives in her hometown of Nashua, New Hampshire, with her husband, Douglas. She pursues an active interest in music, having sung and played guitar professionally for many years until painting took over her life. She now sings just for fun. Deanne is also an amateur photographer and avid gardener. She finds inspiration for many of her paintings from her flower garden.

Table of Contents

Introduction

The History of Decorative Painting

When I began looking into the history of decorative painting, I realized it was going to be impossible to pin down the beginnings of this art form. The further I looked into the origins of decorative painting, the more apparent it became that humankind's desire to decorate our surroundings probably began about the same time we became self-aware. Decorative painting encompasses thousands of styles and histories, from the beautiful Paleolithic cave paintings at Lascaux, France, to the magnificent ceiling of the Sistine Chapel in Rome, and from the simple peasant painting of Germany to the exquisitely refined English Chippendale style. Decorative painting is interwoven with all the decorative arts, including wood carving, metal working, weaving, pottery, jewelry making and all other types of ornamental handicrafts. Each craft and style has evolved and been influenced by the life, times and history of the artisans.

The Baroque acanthus wood carving in Norway influenced the development of Rosemaling in the eighteenth century. Prior to the 1700s, most painting in Norway was confined to churches and the homes of wealthy merchants. The beautiful, swirling wood carvings evolved into sweeping, graceful, painted designs that were first seen in the Telemark region of Norway. From there many other regional styles of painting developed, such as Hallingdal, Stesdal and Rogaland. The Rogaland style seems to have had more European influence with its vases, flowers and tulips. It is rendered in a precise manner and is commonly seen with dark backgrounds, bright contrasts in color and symmetrical designs.

In Sweden, decorative painting also became popular during the 1700s. Two areas known for their wall paintings were Halland in the south and Dalarna in central Sweden. Dalmåning, as the paintings of the Dalarna region are called, is characterized by biblical themes and stylized arrangements of fantasy flowers. Just as in Norway, the folk painters wanted to imitate the paintings in the churches and homes of the wealthy.

The folk art painting of Germany is known as Bauernmalerei. It originated in the mountainous regions of Germany and was originally developed to protect the softwood furniture that was being built by cabinetmakers of that time. Over the years, this painting evolved from *faux* finishes that imitated hardwood furniture to elaborate designs that incorporated fanciful flowers, scrolls and landscapes. This type of painting is typified by its fresh, unsophisticated style and bright colors. Bauernmalerei is ordinarily glazed with some type of antiquing that softens the designs.

In Holland there is Assendelfter and Hinderloopen; in France there is everything from a rustic form of ceramic art called faience, developed in the fifteenth century, to the elaborate and sophisticated painted decoration and gilding during the reigns of Louis XIV and XV. French decorative painting became influential throughout Europe during the 1700s and 1800s. Some of the beautiful floral designs on hand-painted trays from the St. Petersburg and Zhostovo regions in Russia were inspired by the French decorative work of that period.

Every region of the world has its own history and traditions of decorative art. As decorative painters, we are following in a long line of footsteps that traces the history of mankind. Our art form adapts and changes with each new generation of painters. It is a special joy to me to be part of such a long and diverse cultural tradition.

Roses in Decorative Art

One common motif in almost all forms of decorative painting is the rose. Roses have a long and complex history that has been represented in the arts for thousands of years. The first roses were cultivated in China more than five thousand years ago! Some of the earliest known representations of roses are found on the ancient frescoes in the palace at Knossos on Crete. During medieval times, roses were often depicted in tapestries and illuminated manuscripts. They were found in paintings of the Madonna, symbolizing her purity. In English heraldry, the Tudor rose symbolized the union of the red rose of the Lancasters and the white rose of the Yorks.

Today we still feature roses in much of our decorative artwork. Roses can be found on wallpaper, bedspreads, furniture, curtains, rugs and almost any home furnishing you can think of. Their beautiful form and colors make attractive and pleasing additions to our surroundings. I have a small rose garden in my yard by the front steps that has been a source of joy and inspiration to me for many years. I have always loved these beautiful, fragrant blossoms, so it has been a special pleasure for me to write a book dedicated completely to the rose—the queen of flowers. 🙣

Chapter One

Supplies and Preparation

Finding a Work Space

The only way to learn how to paint successfully is to take the time to practice on a regular basis. Just as learning to play a piano or any muscial instrument takes a commitment to practice, learning to paint well takes an equal amount of dedication. One of the best ways to insure that you will make time to paint is to find a dedicated work space. If you have to paint on the kitchen table in between meals, you won't be inclined to paint as often. If you find a space to call your own where you can leave your paints and palette set up, you can pick up your brushes even when you only have a few minutes to spare.

Surfaces

One of the delights of being a decorative painter is that there is such a large range of marvelous surfaces on which to paint. The most common is wood, which comes in as many different shapes and sizes as there are imaginative people to design new boxes, shelves, cabinets, etc. Wooden surfaces can be purchased through many catalogs and crafts shops. Painters generally work on softwoods, because they are less expensive than hardwoods and the grain of the wood will be covered with painting. When shop-

Surfaces
This is a small sampling of the wide variety of wood, tin, stoneware, porcelain and papier-mâché surfaces available for decorative painters.

ping for wood pieces, look for items that are well made and sanded smooth. If a piece of wood is rough and splintery, it will take you a lot of extra time to prepare.

Tin pieces can be purchased in many shapes as well. There are coffeepots, document boxes, lamps . . . almost anything you can think of. Tin pieces can be purchased already primed, or found at garage sales and flea markets and fixed up. If you prefer old pieces, try to find items that are not too banged up and rusted or you'll

probably spend more time fixing them than painting on them.

There are lovely porcelain and stoneware pieces also available that require very little prep work. Some of the stoneware comes with a food-safe glaze on the inside. In my kitchen, I have a delightful little pitcher on which I painted strawberries.

Another readily available, inexpensive surface is papier-mâché. This also comes in hundreds of different shapes, from nesting boxes to large pumpkins.

Preparing Your Surface

One of the hallmarks of an heirloom decorative piece is that it has had attention lavished on every detail from start to finish. With acrylics, it seems there are as many ways of preparing pieces as there are teachers. What can never be shortchanged with a wood piece is proper preparation before applying any sealer or basecoat. A beautiful painting will never cover up a rough or sloppily basecoated piece. Some wood pieces arrive in beautiful condition ready to be sealed; however, this is not the norm. I find that in most cases I have to sand the wood piece before doing anything else to it. I ordinarily use medium (100) grit sandpaper and a sanding block, available at any hardware store.

To begin, cut your sandpaper and place it in the sanding block. Sand the flat surfaces of the wood piece, *with* the direction of the grain, until they are smooth to the touch. Be careful of hand-sanding without a block or you can inadvertently round off the corners of boxes or routed edges. Many painters today use the handy electric palm sanders, but take care with these as well. Be certain not to leave the

sander in one spot for too long or you will sand a depression in the wood. If the edge of a board has some intricate curves, I find it helpful to roll a small piece of sandpaper around a pencil or dowel and use this to sand in the tight places. To get into the corners of a routed edge, I fold a small piece of sandpaper in half and use the folded edge to reach the corners. Make very sure to sand all the routed edges well, even though it can take a lot of extra time. This is where extra care and attention will give you a more polished, finished product. When the piece is nicely sanded, use a tack cloth to pick up all the sanding dust. Now you are ready to seal and basecoat your wood.

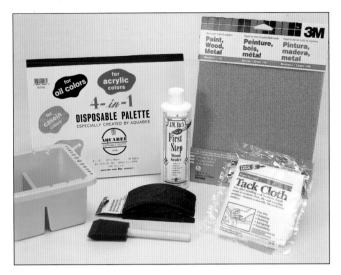

Surface Preparation Supplies
To prepare a wood piece, you will need medium grit sandpaper, a sanding block and a tack cloth. Because wood is porous, the grain will rise, creating a rough surface if you don't seal it first. To seal the wood, you will need a sponge brush, brush basin, waxed palette and wood sealer.

Sealing and Basecoating

Make a mix of equal parts of sealer plus whatever color you want to paint your piece, and with a sponge brush use this mix to seal the wood piece. This will seal and color the wood all in one step. Make sure to always seal both sides and all the edges of a piece to prevent warping. If you seal only one side, the unsealed surface can absorb or lose moisture and will cause the piece to warp and eventually crack. Next, lightly sand the wood (the sealer will raise the grain a little) and then use the tack cloth again to pick up the

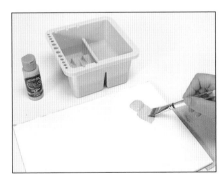

Basecoating

1 Load the paint on the brush and dress the brush on the waxed palette to make sure the paint is evenly loaded in the brush.

2 Paint the surface of the object using a slip-slap motion of the brush.

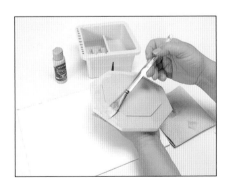

3 When painting against an edge, hold the brush as horizontal to the surface as possible to prevent the paint from flowing over the edge.

sanding dust. Don't oversand the piece as this can reduce the surface tooth and prevent good adhesion between the layers of paint. Then use a large flat brush—I use a Winsor & Newton 1-inch (25mm) flat—to basecoat the piece with the acrylic color you have chosen for your basecoat. Anytime you are basecoating, carry enough moisture in the brush to enable the paint to flow well from the brush. If you start getting unattractive ridges in the paint, you aren't carrying enough water in the brush.

Blended Backgrounds

A lovely background can be achieved by blending value changes into the background color. To accomplish this, seal and basecoat the wood according to the previous instructions. When the basecoat is thoroughly dry, dampen the surface with clean water, then basecoat the area to be blended with the basecoat color thinned with water. While this is still wet, pick up a lighter value and begin to blend into the wet basecoat using slip-slap motions of the brush. I like to use a ¾-inch (19mm) filbert mop brush, but you can also use a ¾-inch (19mm) flat. Start the highlighting on one side of the surface, working toward the opposite side. Now, pick up a darker value and work this into the wet basecoat starting on the shadow side, working toward the highlight side. By predampening the surface and basecoating with thinned color, you have plenty of time to wet-on-wet blend the background. See pages 80 and 111 for illustrations of this technique.

Transferring the Pattern

After you have correctly sanded and prepared your piece, you are ready to transfer the pattern. You need to use as much care in tracing and transferring the pattern as you used when preparing the surface. I can't stress enough to be as accurate as you possibly can when tracing the pattern. If you make a mistake tracing a circle, you will compound the mistake when you transfer the pattern, and by the time you paint the shape, it will probably look like a flattened oval!

Place a clean sheet of tracing paper over the pattern you want to transfer. Use a sharp pencil to trace all the major design lines in the pattern so you can easily erase and correct any mis-

takes. A kneaded eraser is best for removing excess graphite lines. Center the tracing over the prepared piece and tape it lightly but securely in place so that it doesn't shift while you transfer the pattern. Next, slip a piece of graphite paper, graphite side down, between the piece and the tracing paper. Use white graphite paper on dark surfaces and gray on light surfaces. Using a stylus or a dried-out ballpoint pen, trace over the lines. Always trace the lines as lightly as possible. When transferring a folk art design with stroke work, trace a single line down the middle of the stroke instead of the whole outline of the stroke.

Carefully lift the corner of the tracing and check that all lines are visible before you remove the tape. Now you're ready to begin the painting.

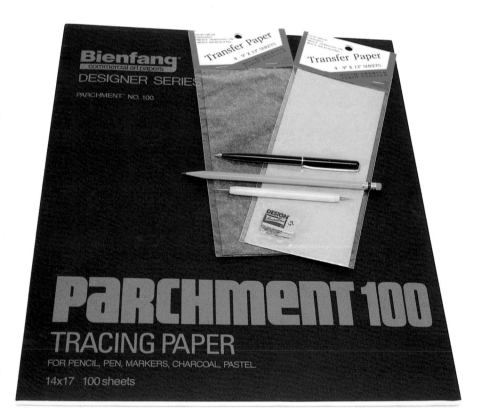

Supplies for Transferring a Pattern
You will need a sharp pencil and tracing paper to trace the design and graphite paper and a stylus or dried-out ballpoint pen to transfer the design to your surface. A kneaded eraser is good for removing excess graphite lines.

Painting Roses With Deanne Fortnam

Brushes

There are hundreds of different acrylic brushes in many different shapes and sizes on the market for the decorative artist. Acrylic brushes are generally made of synthetic fibers, because they hold up better with the acrylics. When buying brushes, look for short handles, as they are easier to use with decorative art techniques.

Round brushes come in sizes ranging from a large no. 12 through a no. 10/0. They can be used for strokework and basecoating small- to medium-sized areas. I use a Winsor & Newton series 520, no. 0 round for detailing.

Flat brushes range from a large 1½-inch (38mm) brush down to a no. 0 and can be used for side loading and basecoating. The flat brush is my workhorse; I use them all the time for side-loaded shading and highlighting. I usually work with Winsor & Newton series 500, sizes no. 4 through no. 14, as well as Winsor & Newton series 995, sizes ¾-inch (19mm) and 1-inch (25mm) flats.

Filberts are sort of a cross between a flat and a round brush. The bristles come out flat from the ferrule but form a curved outline at the end of the brush. The larger filberts are wonderful for blending backgrounds. I also use filberts for side loading when I don't want to create a hard edge. They range from a 1-inch (25mm) down to a no. 2. I use a Loew-Cornell series 7600, ¾-inch (19mm) filbert for blending backgrounds. I also use a Loew-Cornell series 7500, no. 10 and Winsor & Newton series 550, sizes no. 4 through no. 8.

Liner brushes are longer than round brushes and hold more paint. They run from a no. 6 through a no. 10/0. I use Loew-Cornell series 7350, no. 4 and no. 6, for pulling comma strokes.

Script liners are very long and thin, holding a lot of paint so you don't have to reload the brush as often. I use a Loew-Cornell series 7050, size no. 10/0, and a Winsor & Newton series 530, size no. 00.

Angle brushes are very useful for pulling petals on stroke roses and also come in a large range of sizes. I use Loew-Cornell series 7400, sizes ¼-inch (6mm), ⅜-inch (10mm) and ½-inch (13mm).

I also use a ⅜-inch (10mm) Betty Byrd series 410 deerfoot brush for stippling and a ¼-inch (6mm) Loew-Cornell series 7800 dagger brush for striping.

Sable brushes aren't generally recommended for acrylic paints because acrylics are very hard on the sable hairs; however, there are a few applications where the sables are a better tool for the techniques. I used Yarka Kolinsky sables no. 3 and no. 4 for the brushwork on the Russian box, a Winsor & Newton series 7, no. 2 round sable for pulling the Norwegian teardrop strokes on the Norwegian trunk and a Winsor & Newton series 12, no. 4, for the fine stippling on the Norwegian trunk.

Brushes
Acrylic brushes for the decorative artist come in a wide variety of shapes and sizes for many different uses: Use flats for basecoating and side loading, filbert brushes for strokework, basecoating, side loading and blending, script liners and dagger brushes for pulling lines, and rounds and liners for strokework and line work.

Paints

Acrylics were introduced only a few decades ago. They have met with enormous popularity because of their tremendous versatility. They can be thinned down with water and used like a watercolor, mixed with a retarding medium and used to blend wet-on-wet, or because of their fast drying time, the artist can easily build value changes through successive layers of glazing. I primarily work with this last method. I love being able to build my values and adjust the painting however I wish and, unlike with watercolors, I don't have to worry about disturbing the layers underneath, or worry if the surface is dry as with oils.

Acrylics can be purchased in tubes, jars or bottles. There are many good brands of acrylic paint on the market today for the decorative artist. I am currently working with DecoArt Americana bottled acrylics as they come in a wide range of colors and are the perfect consistency for my decorative painting techniques.

Paints
DecoArt Americana bottled acrylics come in a wide range of colors and are the perfect consistency for my painting techniques.

Painting Supplies

You will need a small, trowel-like palette knife, a waxed palette for blending your side loads and double loads and a Sta-Wet palette for keeping your paint workable. A water basin is essential for rinsing your brushes and picking up clean water to paint with. I recommend one of the basins designed with a washboard surface in the bottom for cleaning your brushes, and brush holders molded right into the sides. You will also need a small spray bottle to mist your palette with clean water. Good quality paper towels are a must for absorbing the excess water from your brushes, as well as for placing in your Sta-Wet palette. They are also handy for cleaning your palette knife and wiping up any spills. I use Scott shop towels and Scott rags. They are superabsorbent and last a lot longer than other paper towels.

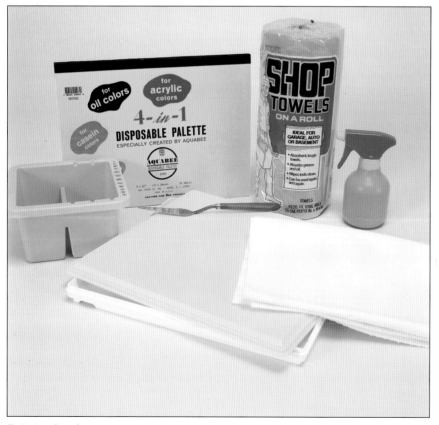

Painting Supplies
You will need a Sta-Wet palette, a waxed palette, palette knife, brush basin, paper towels and a mister bottle.

Painting Roses With Deanne Fortnam

Setting Up Your Palette

1 Soak fresh, white paper towels in clean water and squeeze out the excess moisture. Place two or three layers of paper towel in the bottom of a Sta-Wet palette.

2 If you need to mix colors, mix them with your palette knife on your waxed palette and then transfer them to your Sta-Wet palette. Place your colors from light to dark on the paper toweling.

3 Mist your paints regularly while you are painting to keep them workable.

Supplies for Finishing Techniques

You will need an inexpensive compass and ruler for marking guidelines for striping. Masking tape is handy if you want to band a piece with a different color than the basecoat. I use an old toothbrush and a straightedge palette knife for spattering and a common cellulose kitchen sponge cut into a 2″-diameter (5.1cm) circle for sponging. If you wish to smoke a piece, you will need a candle and an old palette knife. For gold leafing, you will need gold leaf and gold leaf adhesive. To antique your pieces, you will need Raw Umber and Burnt Umber artist's oil paints and Winsor & Newton Blending and Glazing medium. Instructions for these finishing techniques are given on pages 124-126.

Finishing
You will need a compass, ruler, masking tape, old toothbrush, straightedge palette knife, cellulose sponge, scissors, candle, old palette knife, gold leaf, gold leaf adhesive, Raw Umber and Burnt Umber artist's oil paint, and Winsor & Newton Blending and Glazing medium.

Varnishing
You will need an acrylic varnish, a synthetic one-stroke brush, 0000 grade steel wool, a tack cloth, furniture paste wax and a cheesecloth.

Varnishing Supplies

When you are finished with your piece, you can apply a water-based acrylic brush-on varnish. I use JW's Right Step matte clear varnish. I find it helpful to apply the varnish with a ¾-inch (19mm) or 1-inch (25mm) one-stroke brush. The longer bristles hold more varnish than a regular flat does. To hand-rub the finish, use 0000 steel wool. I usually finish my pieces with a coat of Goddard's Cabinet Maker's wax, or Kiwi neutral shoe polish, applied with cheesecloth. See instructions for varnishing on page 127.

Chapter Two
Painting Techniques

Side Loading

1 Blot the excess water off the brush.

2 Dip one corner of the brush into your paint about one-third of the way across the chisel edge.

3 Blend one side of the brush on your waxed palette until you have a soft gradation of color.

4 Flip the brush over and place the edge with paint back into the paint. Blend the other side of the brush to completely work all the paint into the brush. There should be no heavy blob of paint on the loaded corner of the brush.

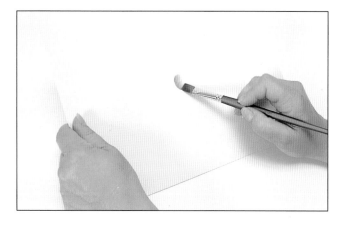

5 Float this side-loaded color on your painting, using small pat-pulls of the brush, holding the brush as horizontal to the surface as possible.

Back-to-Back Side Load

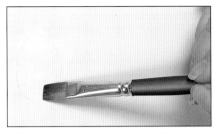

1 Side load your brush, and lightly and evenly dampen the surface with clean water.

2 Side load one side of the line using small pat-pulls of the brush.

3 Flip the brush over and side load the opposite side of the line, softening where the loaded edges overlap.

Bull's-Eye Side Load

1 A bull's-eye is a circular side load that places the heaviest concentration of paint in the center of the circle. To do this you must first side load your brush, and then lightly and evenly dampen the surface. Place the loaded corner of the brush on an imaginary point in the center of the circle.

2 Pull the water-loaded corner of the brush around in a complete circle, keeping the paint-loaded edge of the brush on the center point. Use small pat-pulling motions of the brush to pull this side load around. (If possible, rotate your surface rather than your brush to complete the circle.)

3 A completed bull's-eye side load.

Oval Bull's-Eye Side Load

1 This is a combination of the above side loads. Your goal is to create an oval shape with the heaviest concentration of paint in the center of the oval. Side load your brush and lightly and evenly dampen the surface. Next, visualize the oval shape you want to paint and then imagine a line down the middle of the oval. Side load against one side of this imaginary line.

2 When you get to the end point of the imaginary line, create a half bull's-eye. Next, side load the opposite side of imaginary line, softening where the loaded edges come together.

3 Create another half bull's-eye at the opposite end of the imaginary line until you have completed the oval shape. As with all side loading, you should be working with small pat-pulls of the brush.

Double Loading

1 Blot the excess water from the brush. Tip one corner of the brush into the first color.

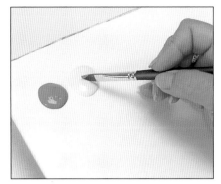

2 Tip the opposite corner of the brush into the second color.

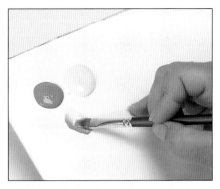

3 Blend the brush on the waxed palette until you have achieved a soft gradation of value between the two colors.

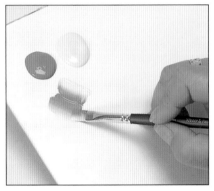

4 Flip the brush and blend the opposite side of the brush on the waxed palette to blend all the paint into the brush.

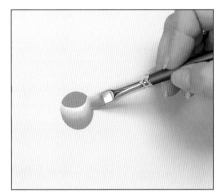

5 The throat of a basic stroke rose can be created using a double-loaded stroke.

Rose Petal Stroke

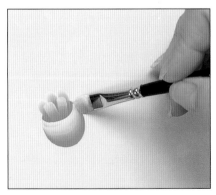

1 Here I have added double-loaded C-strokes to the previous step to create the back center petals of a basic stroke rose. Side load or double load an angle brush. Place the brush against the side of the rose shape. Pull the brush around clockwise to create the top of the petal.

2 Slide the brush to its chisel edge to create the bottom of the petal, turning your work as needed.

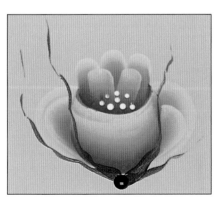

3 A completed basic stroke rose.

Painting Roses With Deanne Fortnam

Comma Stroke

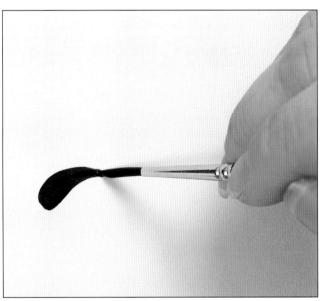

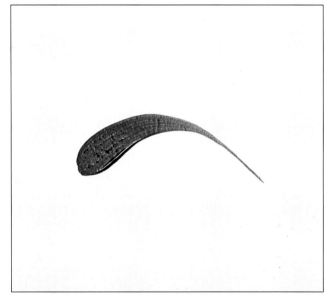

1 Pick up some paint and dress it into the
brush on the waxed palette.

2 Press the brush down to create
the head of the stroke.

3 Begin lifting the brush to create the
elbow of the stroke.

4 Pull the tail of
the stroke.

S-Stroke

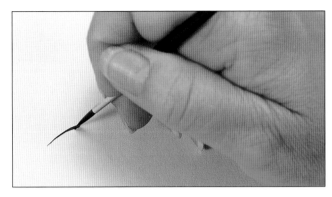

1 Pick up some paint and dress it into the brush on the waxed palette. Flatten the brush to a chisel edge on the waxed palette. Begin the stroke by painting a line with the chisel edge of the brush.

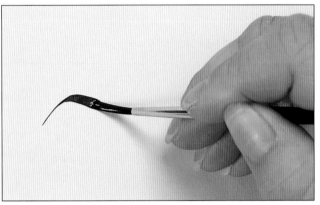

2 Apply pressure and paint the wide part of the stroke.

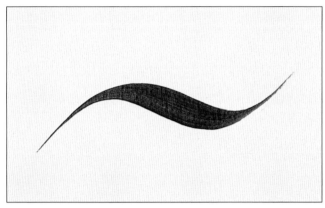

3 Lift the brush and pull the tail of the stroke.

C-Stroke

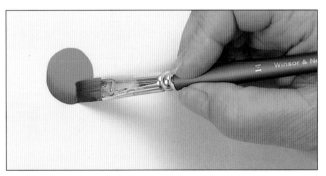

1 Side load or double load the brush and place the brush with the chisel edge against the outside edge of the shape you are painting (in this case, a circle).

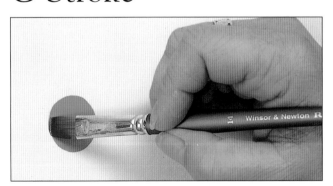

2 Pull the brush in a C-shape following the shape of the object.

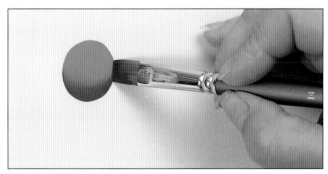

3 Finish with the chisel edge of the brush against the opposite outside edge of the shape.

Painting Roses With Deanne Fortnam

Norwegian Teardrop Stroke

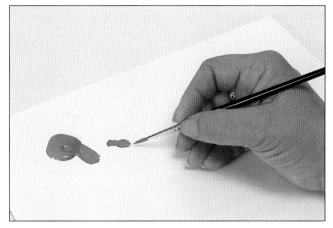

1 Dress the paint into the brush and twirl the brush to a fine point.

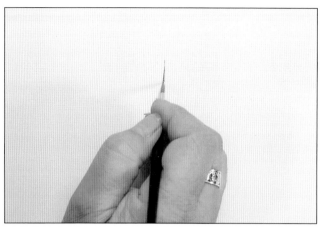

2 Begin the stroke using light pressure on the brush to paint a line that creates the tail of the stroke.

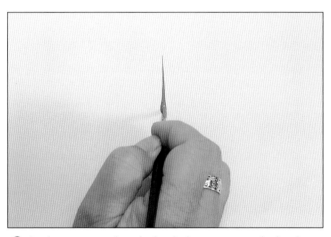

3 Apply pressure and sit the brush down to create the head of the stroke.

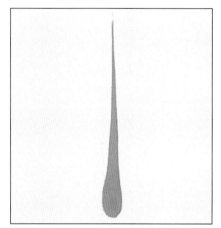

4 The completed teardrop.

Line Work

1 Pick up the desired color on the brush, then pick up some extra water. Brush mix the extra water and paint together on the waxed palette. The paint needs to be the consistency of ink.

2 Hold the brush perpendicular to the surface and pull the lines with light pressure on the brush.

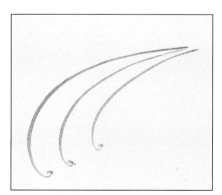

3 Completed line work.

Chapter Three

Step-by-Step Projects

Beginning Rosebuds

*T*his is a charming little set of papier-mâché boxes designed with the beginning painter in mind. These rosebuds are painted using a simple oval shape that can be achieved by anyone at any skill level. This project uses the double-loading technique described on page 16. The design is loosely painted—you can use the patterns provided or freehand the design on a piece of your choice. The sponging adds a special touch to the lids of the boxes and is easily accomplished. Whether you are a veteran painter or just starting out, I know you will find these rosebuds fun to paint!

Preparation

Largest and Smallest Boxes

You will be preparing both the largest and smallest heart boxes in the same manner. Begin by basecoating the tops of the lids with Green Mist. It will take two or more coats of paint to achieve opaque coverage. Let this dry. Next, using your sponge as described on page 125, texture against the outside edges on top of the lids with Deep Teal. When you are finished with the spon-

ging, you can Paint the edges of the lids with Deep Teal. Now basecoat the sides of the boxes with Taupe. When this is dry, load a no. 4 flat with Deep Teal, then tap the brush on the waxed palette to remove any excess paint. Using even pressure all the way around the box, paint a band of Deep Teal the width of the brush against the bottom edge of the box. Make sure there is no ridge of paint at the edge of the band; this would mean that you are carrying too much paint in the brush.

Medium Box

Begin preparing the medium heart box by basecoating the top of the lid with Taupe. Next, sponge around the outside edge of the top of the lid with Deep Teal and paint the side of the box with Green Mist. To finish the preparation work, paint a band of Deep Teal the width of a no. 4 flat against the bottom edge of the box. You are now ready to transfer the patterns found on page 26 to your boxes. When this is done, you are ready to paint! Follow the easy step-by-step illustrations to paint these beginning rosebuds.

Materials

Palette
DecoArt Americana acrylic paints
- Antique Teal
- Black Green
- Deep Teal
- Green Mist
- Light Buttermilk
- Raspberry
- Taupe

Surface
This set of papier-mâché nesting heart boxes can be purchased from Viking Woodcrafts, Inc., 1317 Eighth Street SE, Waseca, MN 56093. (507) 835-8043.

Brushes
To paint this project, you will need a wide bristle or sponge brush for basecoating the boxes, a no. 4 filbert, a no. 4 flat and a 10/0 script liner.

Miscellaneous
You will need a kitchen sponge, cut into a 2"-diameter (5.1cm) circle.

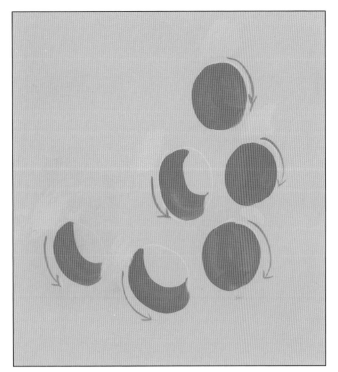

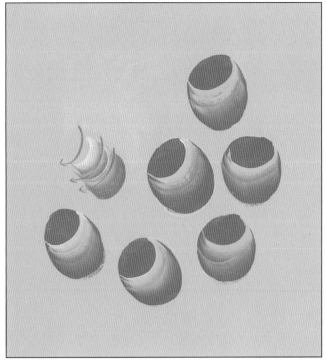

1 Basecoat the ovals that form the rosebuds with a no. 4 filbert loaded with Raspberry. Paint the ovals with two shape following strokes.

2 Load a no. 4 flat with Raspberry, then tip one corner of the brush in Light Buttermilk. Blend the brush by stroking on the waxed palette until you have a smooth blend of color from the Raspberry to the Light Buttermilk. Paint a series of C-strokes with the Light Buttermilk side of the brush facing the top of the rosebuds. The first stroke will be against the throat or top of the rose, then paint overlapping strokes moving the brush down toward the bottom of the oval. Stop when the Raspberry corner of the brush is against the bottom of the buds. This can take anywhere from two to four C-strokes.

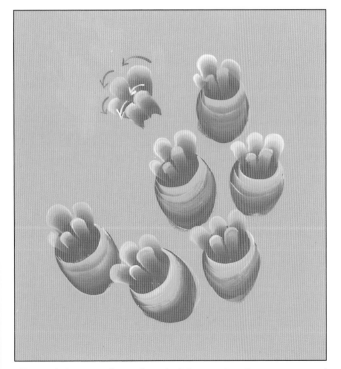

3 Load the no. 4 flat as described for step 2 and paint a series of C-strokes to create the upper petals. These should again be painted with the Light Buttermilk edge of the brush facing up.

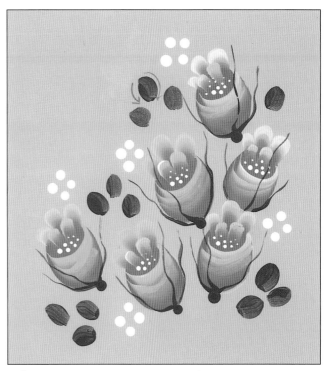

4 Load a 10/0 script liner with Antique Teal. Starting at the base of the rosebud, pull an irregular line to form the calyxes. Make these lines taper to a fine point. Place a large dot of Antique Teal at the bases of the rosebuds using the handle end of the script liner. Reload the handle after each application to create evenly sized dots. Place a series of small, Light Buttermilk dots in the throats of the rosebuds using the small end of a stylus. Complete all the dots in one rosebud before reloading the handle, to create a variety of dot sizes.

5 Paint small oval leaf shapes with a no. 4 filbert loaded with Antique Teal. Make small dot flowers with the handle end of a small brush loaded with Light Buttermilk, reloading after each application for evenly sized petals.

6 Place a dot of Raspberry in the center of each dot flower. Pull stems and lines with a mixture of 1 part Black Green + 1 part Antique Teal, using a 10/0 script liner.

Yellow Rosebuds

Preparation

Seal and sand the wooden lids. Base-coat the tops of the lids with Taupe. Sponge around the outside edges of the lids with Green Mist. Paint the curved edges of the lids with Deep Teal. When this is dry, you can transfer the patterns.

Painting Procedure

The yellow roses are painted in the same manner as described for the Beginning Rosebuds in project 1. Substitute True Ochre for Raspberry for the rosebuds and the centers of the dot flowers. Paint the leaves with Deep Teal instead of Antique Teal. Paint the white blossoms on this pattern with a no. 4 filbert loaded with Light Buttermilk. Place the brush at the outside edge of the petal and pull toward the center. Place a large brush handle dot of True Ochre in the center of each flower.

Materials

Palette
DecoArt Americana acrylic paints
- Antique Teal
- Black Green
- Deep Teal
- Green Mist
- Light Buttermilk
- Taupe
- True Ochre

Surface
These two glass bowls with wooden lids can be purchased from Covered Bridge Crafts, 449 Amherst Street, Nashua, NH 03063. (800) 405-4464.

Brushes
To paint this project you will need a ¾-inch (19mm) flat for basecoating the boxes, a no. 4 filbert, a no. 4 flat and a 10/0 script liner.

Miscellaneous
A kitchen sponge cut into a 2″-diameter (5.1cm) circle.

Mix pink and yellow rosebuds and the two types of blossoms to create colorful, delicate designs that will grace any surface.

Detail of large heart box lid

Pattern for medium heart box

Pattern for small heart box

Pattern for large heart box

Border for sides of heart boxes

Detail of octagonal lid

These patterns (pages 26-27) may be hand-traced or photocopied for personal use only.

Pattern for small glass bowl

Pattern for octagonal bowl

Painting Roses With Deanne Fortnam

Basic Stroke Roses

$\mathcal{T}$his little design uses the comma stroke, the basis for many decorative designs. When you are learning to paint comma strokes, don't expect to paint every one perfectly. It takes a good deal of practice to have all your strokes come out gracefully. Painting comma strokes is a wonderful exercise for learning brush control (and patience). Resist the impulse to wipe off the strokes you don't like; eventually your background will get smudged and messy looking. Even if all the strokes are not perfect, the final painting will still be pretty.

This project also uses side loading, which is the backbone of most high-lighting and shading in acrylics. We will be using it here to shade the roses and the bases of the leaves. Take the time to blend the brush properly on your palette and you will see softer results on your painting. If you are a beginning painter, you will probably find it helpful to practice a few of these roses on scrap paper or illustration board before putting them on your box.

Preparation

Begin this project by sanding the box well, inside and out. Clean up all the sanding dust with a tack cloth. Seal the box inside and out with an acrylic wood sealer and let it dry well. When the box is thoroughly dry, sand and tack it again if necessary. Make very sure that you have removed all the sanding dust before basecoating. Sometimes it's easier to use a vacuum to clean the inside of the box.

Basecoat the box and lid inside and out with Buttermilk. You don't need to paint the green and mauve areas on the top of the box and edge of the lid at this time. To add the texturing, dampen and crumple up a piece of heavy-duty paper towel. Pick up a thin amount of Cool Neutral on the crumpled paper towel. Lightly press this color onto the sides of the box and the top of the lid, creating a nice, even texture. Repeat this technique with Titanium White. When doing this type of texturing, make sure you're not building up heavy ridges of paint on the surface. When the texturing is dry, transfer your pattern to the box. Remember that the more accurate you are when you transfer your pattern, the better your final painting will be!

Materials

Palette

DecoArt Americana acrylic paints
- Alizarin Crimson
- Antique Mauve
- Black Forest Green
- Buttermilk
- Cool Neutral
- Jade Green
- Light Avocado
- Midnite Green
- Titanium (Snow) White

Surface

This small, octagonal wooden box can be purchased from Covered Bridge Crafts, 449 Amherst Street, Nashua, NH 03063. (800) 405-4464.

Brushes

To paint this project you will need a wide bristle or sponge brush for base-coating the box, a no. 4 or no. 6 filbert, a no. 4 and a no. 6 liner (I use Loew-Cornell 7350 series), a 10/0 script liner and no. 8 through no. 12 flats.

Miscellaneous

You will need a heavy-duty paper towel for texturing the box. I use Scott rags.

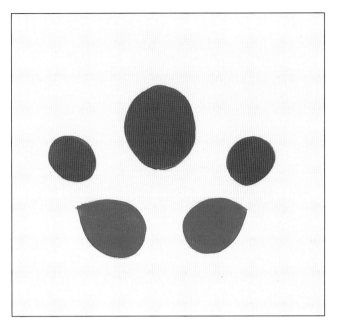

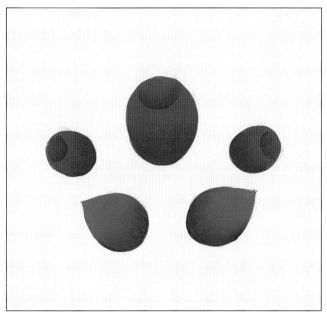

1 Basecoat the large and small roses with Antique Mauve and the leaves with Light Avocado. You want to get smooth, opaque coverage and avoid building up a ridge of paint on the outside edges of the shapes.

2 Side load a no. 12 flat brush with Alizarin Crimson and shade against the base and throat of the large roses. Shade the small roses in the same manner, using a smaller brush to fit the area you are working on. Side load a no. 12 flat brush with Black Forest Green and shade against the base of the leaves.

3 Make a mix of equal parts of Antique Mauve and Alizarin Crimson. With a no. 6 liner, pull a comma stroke on either side of the large roses from the throat to the bottom of the roses. Pull a second comma stroke outside the first strokes. Reinforce the shading on the leaves with a no. 8 flat brush side loaded with Midnite Green.

4 Make a mix of equal parts of Antique Mauve and Titanium White. With a no. 6 liner, pull a series of horizontal comma strokes starting from the throat of the roses toward the base. You will need three to five comma strokes here, depending on how large your strokes come out. Pull one more horizontal stroke on the top of each rose, starting the comma's head on the opposite side of the previous strokes. For the smaller roses you may want to use the no. 4 liner instead of the no. 6. With your 10/0 script liner, pull lines of Jade Green from the tips of the leaves.

5 Overstroke the commas on the oval section of the large roses with Titanium White on your no. 4 liner. Pull Midnite Green stem and vein lines with your 10/0 script liner.

6 Place small, uneven dots of Titanium White in the throats of the roses. Place large Titanium White dots at the bases of the small roses, reloading after each application. Pull comma strokes of Antique Mauve and a mix of Antique Mauve plus Titanium White on either side of the large roses.

Paint the filler leaves with a liner or small round brush and Midnite Green. Pick up a generous amount of paint on the end of the brush, set it down on your surface and pull the brush to the side. You can add these leaves wherever you wish in the design.

Finishing the Box

Banding

It's always nice to pick up colors from the palette and create contrasting banding and striping to add more visual interest. I first painted the routed edge of the lid with a band of Antique Mauve, then Light Avocado and last with Midnite Green. I painted the upper section of the box with Light Avocado, then used Antique Mauve in the routed groove. You can re-arrange the colors however you like; just be sure to pick colors from the ex-isting palette.

Rose Border

The rose border on the bottom edge of the box is painted in the same manner as the design on the lid. The only new item in this border is the small stroke leaf shown on page 32. I recommend that you practice a few of these on your waxed palette before you put them on your box. Like any type of stroke ele-ment, it takes a little practice to feel comfortable. If you don't succeed at first, don't get discouraged. Have patience with yourself and you will succeed!

Strokework Border

Strokework borders make an attractive trim. You can paint a border as simple as a single line of comma strokes, or combine striping, comma strokes, dots and S-strokes to make an interesting design. Choose colors from your main design elements to harmonize with the painting, or paint a contrasting border like the gold borders on project 7. On this project I added a simple strokework border to the bottom of the box and to the inside of the lid. Placing little details like these where they are least expected—on the bottom of a box or the back of a piece—gives your piece extra charm.

This detail shows the rose border on the sides of the box, as well as the strokework borders on the bottom of the box and on the inside of the lid (right).

1 Double load a no. 4 filbert with Light Avocado and Midnite Green. Set the brush down at the base of the leaf.

2 In one motion, lift the brush and pull it up to its chisel edge. This will create the pointed tip of the leaf.

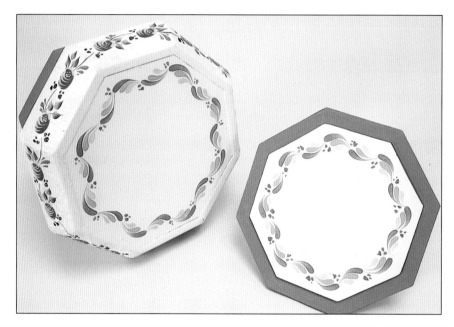

1 Mark an erasable guideline. You can use a soapstone, chalk or graphite pencil. Paint a row of comma strokes alternating above and below the line with a no. 6 liner and Light Avocado.

2 Erase the line. Paint a smaller comma stroke inside each of the Light Avocado strokes with Jade Green.

3 Paint an even smaller comma stroke inside the Jade Green comma strokes with a mixture of Jade Green plus some Titanium White.

4 Paint some filler Antique Mauve berry shapes at the head of each of the Light Avocado comma strokes.

Painting Roses With Deanne Fortnam

Pattern for rose border

Pattern for top of lid

These patterns may be hand-traced or photocopied for personal use only.

Detail of lid

A Rosy Picture Album

T his is a lovely and useful little photo album that would be pretty on your coffee table or on a bookshelf to display your favorite photographs. The canvas cover is a new and interesting surface for you to try painting on. You will probably find it a little more challenging than painting on wood because there is more texture to deal with; however, the fabric enables you to effortlessly create a soft, watercolor-like background.

When I'm working on a canvas surface, I find it helps to lightly dampen the shapes I'm about to paint. This helps the paint work into the fabric and reduces the dragging that occurs while working on a dry canvas background. Make sure not to use too much water or go outside the leaf or rose shapes when you predampen or the color might bleed outside the design lines.

These roses and leaves are easily painted using the skills you have already learned: side loading, double loading, C-strokes and comma strokes. Review the two previous projects if you're unsure of any of these techniques. The more you practice, the faster you'll learn. The roses in this design, like those in the previous projects, begin with oval shapes. In this lesson, however, you will be building more complicated roses by adding petals to both sides of the ovals, using a double-loaded angle brush. As with anything new, practice a few of these

roses on a piece of scrap paper or illustration board before you paint on your surface. This is especially important on this canvas background—since there is no basecoat, you can't paint over any mistakes! Enjoy the design and get creative. Try changing the line drawing to fit a variety of different pieces. Most of all, have fun!

Preparation

Thoroughly wet the front surface of the book with clean water and a ¾-inch (19mm) filbert mop. Begin applying thinned Hauser Dark Green with the ¾-inch (19mm) filbert using slip-slap motions of the brush. Begin in the lower left corner and work toward the upper right corner, letting the color fade into the background in the center. Now work the color from the upper right corner toward the lower left corner, again letting the color fade into the background in the center of the cover. Let this dry thoroughly overnight, then transfer the pattern.

If you decide to use this pattern on a wood piece, prepare it according to the instructions on page 9 and basecoat it with DecoArt Americana Cool Neutral or Eggshell. The pattern will easily fit an oval shape or could be adapted to fit a larger rectangle by creating a wider gap in the corners where the roses face each other. If you want to make the design fit a

smaller piece, drop the two outermost roses in each corner. When I want to adapt a pattern to fit a different piece, I usually trace the shape of the new piece onto tracing paper. I place this traced outline over the line drawing, and mix and match the design elements until they fit into the new shape. This is a very good pattern for changing and adapting, and I hope you give it a try.

Materials

Palette
DecoArt Americana acrylic paints
- Antique Rose
- Country Red
- Deep Teal
- Hauser Dark Green
- Jade Green
- Midnite Green
- Napa Red
- Titanium (Snow) White

Surface
This 7¾″ × 9″ (19.7cm × 22.9cm) photo album is available from Dalee Bookbinding Co./Creations in Canvas, 129 Clinton Place, Yonkers, NY 10701. (914) 965-1660.

Brushes
To paint this project you will need a ¾-inch (19mm) filbert mop, a no. 8 and a no. 10 flat, a no. 6 and a no. 8 filbert, a no. 00 script liner, a ¼-inch (6mm) angle, a ¼-inch (6mm) dagger and a no. 6 liner.

Painting Procedure

Begin the painting with the roses, next paint the double-loaded leaves, then the shadow leaves, the stems and veins, and last the comma strokes. You should always paint your comma strokes last so you can pull them to flow with the direction of the line work. You can also use commas to fill in any area of the painting that seems a little empty. If the paint is grabbing while you are working on the roses and leaves, remember to lightly dampen the shapes with clean water before you paint them. You can't do this with the comma strokes, however, because the tails of the strokes would bleed into the background. To successfully paint the strokes on this canvas background, carry a little more water in your brush and pull the strokes slowly.

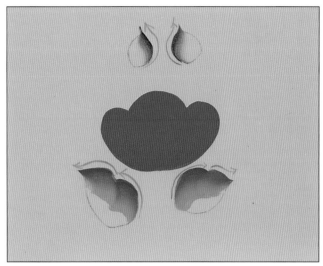

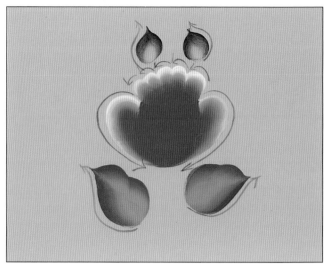

1 Basecoat the oval and two side petals of the roses with Antique Rose. To paint the large blended leaves, double load a no. 8 filbert with Deep Teal and Jade Green. Make sure to have a good blend between the two colors before working on your painting. Place the brush against the base of a leaf with the Deep Teal side against the outside edge. Begin to pull the stroke, pressing the brush down to make the bristles flare out. Follow the outside edge of the leaf, pulling the brush in the direction indicated by the arrows in the illustration. When you get to the tip of the leaf, turn the brush up to its chisel edge to pull the stroke into the point of the leaf. The notched sides of the leaves are pulled in two strokes.

To paint the shadow leaves, side load a no. 6 filbert with Midnite Green. Place the brush against the base of the leaf with the loaded edge against the outside edge of the leaf. Pull the brush in the direction indicated by the arrows in the illustration, bringing the brush up to its chisel edge to pull the stroke into the point of the leaf.

2 Double load a no. 8 flat with Antique Rose and Titanium White. Place the Titanium White edge against the outer ruffled edge and pull a series of C-strokes. Make sure these strokes form a continuous band of color without any spaces between the strokes. Double load a ¼-inch (6mm) angle brush with Antique Rose and Titanium White. The Titanium White should be on the longer, pointed side of the angle brush. Place the brush against the outside edge of the oval with the white against the top of the outside petal. Begin the stroke by applying pressure on the brush; this will flare the Titanium White edge to create the rounded top of the petal. Keeping the Antique Rose corner of the brush against the center oval, pull the petal stroke in the direction of the arrow on the illustration. As you finish the petal stroke, lift the angle brush up onto its chisel edge and slide it against the base of the rose. This should be accomplished in one continuous motion of the brush. The pressure at the beginning of the stroke will round the top of the petal. As you continue the stroke, the lifting of the brush will automatically narrow the stroke until it disappears into the base of the rose.

Double load a no. 8 filbert with Deep Teal and Jade Green and complete the other half of the large, blended leaves, starting at the base of the leaf and lifting the brush to pull the chisel edge into the point of the leaf. To complete the shadow leaves, side load a no. 6 filbert with Midnite Green and pull a second stroke from the base to the tip of the leaf.

Painting Roses With Deanne Fortnam

If you lose the dark green on the outside edge of the leaf, you are not lifting your brush soon enough.

If you have a hole in the center of the leaves, you are not using enough pressure at the beginning of the stroke.

3 Double load a no. 8 flat with Antique Rose and Titanium White and pull the second band of C-strokes to form the inner ruffled edge. Double load a ¼-inch (6mm) angle brush with Antique Rose and Titanium White and pull a smaller petal stroke inside the previously pulled stroke on either side, in the same manner as described for step 2.

4 Double load a no. 10 flat with Antique Rose and Titanium White. Place the Titanium White against the bottom edge of the throat of the rose and pull a large C-stroke to highlight the edge.

5 Again, double load a no. 10 flat with Antique Rose and Titanium White. Place the Titanium White edge slightly below the highlight you just created and pull a second C-stroke.

6 Side load a no. 10 flat with Country Red, and shade in the throat and against the base of the rose.

7 Side load a no. 8 flat with Napa Red, and reinforce the shading in the throat and against the base of the rose.

8 Use a no. 00 script liner loaded with thinned Midnite Green to pull all the lines, stems and veins. Load a no. 6 liner with Napa Red or Country Red and pull the comma strokes. Place Titanium White brush handle dots in the throats and at the bases of the roses.

Finishing

If you wish you can add some striping to the binding of the album. I added a Midnite Green stripe ⅜-inch (1cm) from the edges, then painted a stripe of Napa Red 1/16-inch (0.2cm) inside the Midnite Green. Refer to page 124 for instructions on applying stripes. Finish off the book with several coats of varnish (I used Blair Satin Tole) to protect your painting. Now all that is left is to fill the album with your favorite photographs.

Pattern for album

DEANNE FORTNAM

Bavarian Clock

This charming clock is painted in the Bavarian peasant style called Bauernmalerei. You will be amazed at how quickly you can paint it. You can purchase the lovely clock face and bezel, or paint your own clock face on the wooden board. This style of painting is very free and un-sophisticated, featuring a wet-on-wet technique. Each of the flowers is painted to completion while its base-coat is still wet. This allows for a lovely streaking of colors and creates value changes with the overstroking. As each stroke is added without reloading the brush, the value gets closer to the basecoat of the flower.

The technique is not difficult but does require a bit of practice. I recommend that you practice each of the flower forms following the step-by-step illustrations several times on a practice sheet before you try them on your clock. It's best to be familiar with all the steps for each flower because the overstroking has to be completed quickly, before the basecoat dries.

The best way to paint the roses in this design is to start with the center circles of the roses (or the ovals for the rosebuds) and freehand all the overstroking. These are simple flowers that do not have to be painted perfectly to create a lovely piece. In a short time you will be able to freehand your own designs without a pattern, using the basic flower forms from this clock. This pattern would also look nice painted on a dark blue background, which is a traditional color for this style of painting. Because this style of painting is so quick, it would be a terrific choice for decorating party favors or creating an impromptu gift. Change the colors to suit your taste and get creative. You'll be delighted with how quickly you can have finished pieces with this charming folk art style.

I added some simplified elements from the design to the back of my clock for an extra finishing touch.

Materials

Palette
DecoArt Americana acrylic paints
- Antique Gold
- Antique White
- Black Green
- Deep Midnight Blue
- Deep Teal
- Glorious Gold (Dazzling Metallics)
- Jade Green
- Raspberry
- Rookwood Red
- Shale Green
- Titanium (Snow) White
- Williamsburg Blue

Surface
This wooden clock can be purchased from Covered Bridge Crafts, 449 Amherst Street, Nashua, NH 03063. (800) 405-4464. The 5¾-inch (14.6cm) clock face with hinged bezel can be ordered from Klockit, P.O. Box 636, Lake Geneva, WI 53147-0636. (800) 556-2548.

Brushes
To paint this project, you will need a large flat for basecoating, a Loew-Cornell series 7350, no. 4 and no. 6 liners and a good script liner.

Miscellaneous
To antique the piece, you will need Winsor & Newton artist's oil colors in Burnt Umber and Raw Umber and Winsor & Newton Blending and Glazing Medium.

Preparation

Seal and sand both sides of the clock board. It is very important to sand this piece well, because it will be antiqued after the painting is completed. If the initial sanding is not done well, any imperfection in the wood will show up in the antiquing stage. Basecoat the entire clock board with Antique White. Next mark a line ⅝″ (1.6cm) from the bottom and the top edges of the clock board. (Measure from the edge of the front surface of the clock board, not from the outside routed edge.) Basecoat above the line on the top and below the line on the bottom with Deep Teal. Paint the curving, routed edges with Glorious Gold. When this is thoroughly dry, you can transfer the pattern. With this style of painting it's best to transfer as few lines as possible. The roses can be indicated with a circle and the buds with an oval. There is no need to trace all the lines that indicate the overstrokes.

Painting Procedure

Scrolls

Begin this project by painting the white scrolls at the bottom and top of the design with a no. 6 liner loaded with Titanium White. I usually complete the entire line of scrolls from one side to the other before adding the additional comma overstrokes. The commas over the scrolls are also painted with Titanium White. The best way to achieve a good flow with these overstrokes is to freehand them in without using a pattern. You may wish to practice these a few times before painting them on your clock.

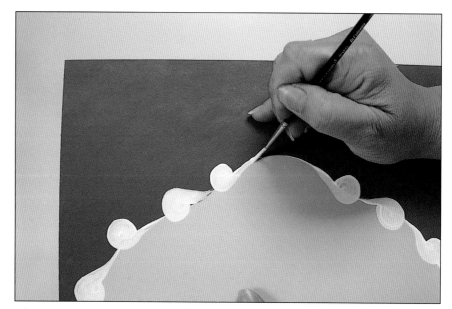

1 Starting in the center of the scroll, press your brush down to flatten out the bristles and pull the brush around in a circle to create the head. Slowly lift the brush to a point as you create the tail of the scroll, following the curve of the clock board. Study the detail on page 51 to position the scrolls; some turn toward the center of the clock and some turn away.

2 Add several comma overstrokes to either side of the tail of each scroll, randomly overlapping the strokes to create a leaflike pattern.

Leaves

You can paint the leaves either before or after you paint the roses. If you paint the leaves first, make sure the roses overlap the bases of the leaves. This is the best way to do it as you won't have to worry about covering the outside overstrokes on the roses; however, if you have trouble getting your roses large enough to cover the bases of the leaves, you can paint the leaves last. Make sure you don't change the shapes of the strokes on the outer rose petals.

Strokes, Lines and Dots

After painting the roses and the leaves, I painted the rosebuds, then the blossoms and last the berries. All the strokes and lines on the background of the design are painted with Black Green. The fillers are painted with Glorious Gold. To paint these, load a small round or liner brush with Glorious Gold, set the brush down on its side and lightly pull it to the side while lifting it off the surface. Make these strokes loose and free. You can paint them wherever you need to fill a space in the design. The dots are all done using a stylus or pencil point dipped in Titanium White. Again, you can paint these wherever you wish to fill in an area of the design.

Clock Face

The clock face I used comes with double brass rings and is white in the center. I decided it would look better if the center was painted to match the design. If you wish to do this, rough up the white paint in the center with steel wool, then cover the area with a light coat of Jo Sonja's All Purpose Sealer. When this is dry, basecoat the center with Antique White, then paint the rosebuds and berries following the step-by-step instructions on pages 46 and 48.

LEAVES

1 Basecoat the leaf shape with a mix of two parts Deep Teal to one part Jade Green.

Palette
- Deep Teal
- Jade Green
- Titanium White
- Black Green

2 Use a no. 4 or no. 6 liner loaded with Titanium White and overstroke one side of the leaf edges.

3 With a script liner and Black Green, line the unfinished side of the leaves. Use a thin-thick-thin line; this looks more graceful than a line of even width. To do this, start with light pressure on the brush when you begin the line, apply more pressure in the middle and again lighten the pressure as you end the line. Still using the script liner and Black Green, paint a thin comma or S-stroke to indicate a vein line in the centers of the leaves, then continue to paint smaller strokes on either side of the center strokes.

ROSES

Palette
- Raspberry
- Rookwood Red
- Titanium White
- Glorious Gold

1 Paint the roses one at a time from beginning to end. Basecoat the large center circle of the rose with a no. 6 liner and Raspberry. Press the brush down to flatten it so that it covers a larger area.

2 While the circle is still wet, wipe your brush on a paper towel to remove the excess paint from the brush. (Don't rinse the brush out; the whole rose should be painted with a "dirty" brush.) Now pick up some Rookwood Red on your flattened brush and paint a C-stroke at the base of the rose. Continue to stroke the brush, walking it further up from the base without rinsing or wiping the brush. The red will be streaked with the Raspberry basecoat and will fade into the basecoat as you paint each successive stroke.

Wipe the brush on a paper towel and reload it with Rookwood Red. Paint a stroke at the top of the circle, outside the basecoated area. Complete an oval shape with a second stroke below the previous one that goes over the wet basecoated circle.

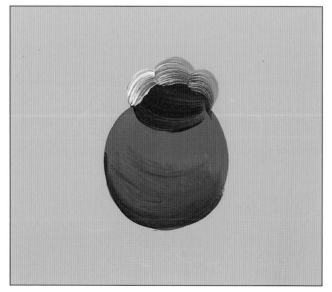

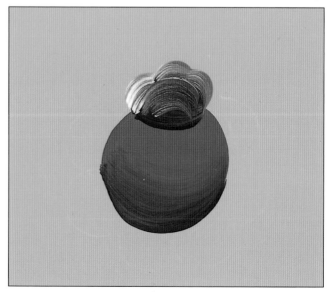

3 Wipe your brush on a paper towel. Again, do not rinse your brush. Using a "dirty" brush adds color and streaking to the overstrokes. Pick up Titanium White and paint three comma strokes on the top of the Rookwood Red oval.

4 Without wiping your brush or picking up more white, pull two more comma strokes overlapping the upper strokes. Notice that the Titanium White is strongest at the outside edge and fades toward the center.

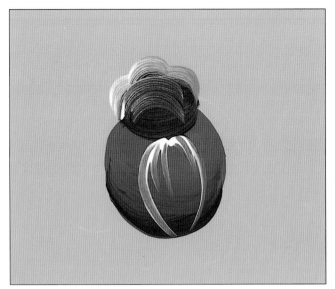

5 Wipe your brush and twirl it to a point on a paper towel. Dip the tip of the brush into Titanium White and pull a long, thin comma stroke from the throat of the rose to the base, starting at the center of the rose. Twirl your brush to a point again, then dip into Titanium White and pull a second stroke. The stroke on the right should curve to the right, and the stroke on the left should curve to the left. Use the tip of your brush to go into the top of the strokes and pull down a few shorter streaks.

6 Continue to twirl the brush, dip into Titanium White, then pull comma strokes from the throat to the base until you finish at the outside edges. Again pull some short streaks from the top of the strokes.

7 Rinse your brush and pick up Raspberry. Pull six thick comma strokes around the outside edge, starting from the top of the rose and painting toward the bottom.

8 Without rinsing your brush, twirl it to a point and load the tip with Titanium White. Overstroke the outside edges of the Raspberry commas, using a fresh load of Titanium White for each one.

Using a small brush handle, place dots of Glorious Gold and Titanium White in the throat of the rose, completing all the dots of one color without reloading the brush handle so that the dots descend in size.

ROSEBUDS

Palette
- Raspberry
- Rookwood Red
- Titanium White
- Deep Teal
- Glorious Gold

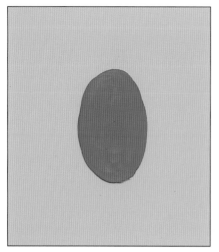

1 Basecoat an oval with a no. 4 liner loaded with Raspberry. Paint only one rosebud at a time.

2 Flatten the brush, load it with Rookwood Red and paint an oval shape on the top with two strokes, as you did for the rose.

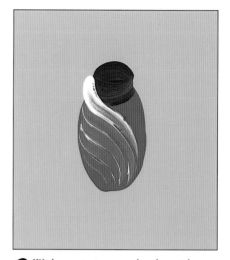

3 Without rinsing your brush, twirl it to a point and load it with Titanium White. Pull an S-stroke from the throat to the base of the bud. The stroke will angle to the right or left depending on where the bud falls in the design. Refer to the photo on page 51 for placement. Without reloading the brush, overlap the original stroke and continue to pull smaller S-strokes below the first until you get to the outside edge of the bud.

4 Without reloading the brush, pull two comma strokes around the Rookwood Red oval at the top of the bud.

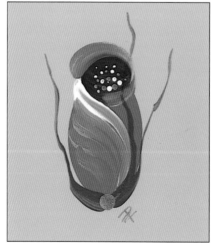

5 Pull the calyxes from the base of the bud with a no. 4 liner loaded with Deep Teal. Place a large Glorious Gold dot at the base of the rosebud. Place small, descending-sized dots of Titanium White and Glorious Gold in the throats of the rosebuds.

BLOSSOMS

Palette
- Shale Green
- Titanium White
- Antique Gold
- Rookwood Red
- Glorious Gold
- Deep Teal
- Black Green

1 Paint only one flower at a time. Load a no. 4 liner with Shale Green and basecoat the flowers.

2 Without rinsing the brush, twirl it to a point and dip the tip in Titanium White. Pull a stroke on either side of each petal shape, then pull streaks from the tips toward the centers. Load the brush once for each petal, creating more streaking and variation in the values of the overstrokes.

3 Rinse your brush and pick up Antique Gold. Basecoat the centers of the five-petal blossoms.

4 Wipe your brush on a paper towel and pick up Rookwood Red. Paint a couple of strokes on the bottoms of the flower centers over the wet Antique Gold to create a shaded area. When this is dry, paint a couple of small Glorious Gold comma strokes on the tops of the blossom centers. Paint a row of descending-sized Titanium White dots against the Rookwood Red shading.

Paint calyxes of Deep Teal with a no. 4 liner on the blossoms that do not have centers. Outline the blossoms and calyxes with a script liner and Black Green. Place dots of Glorious Gold where the calyxes meet the stems on the blossoms without centers.

BERRIES

Palette

- Williamsburg Blue
- Deep Midnight Blue
- Titanium White
- Glorious Gold

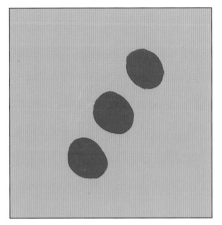

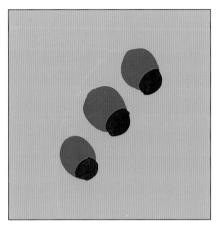

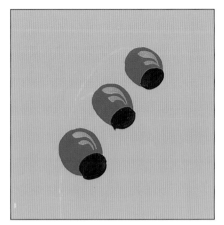

1 Basecoat the berries with Williamsburg Blue.

2 When the basecoat is dry, paint an oval of Deep Midnight Blue on one end of the berries.

3 Brush mix Titanium White with Williamsburg Blue to create a light blue, and pull a couple of small comma strokes on one side of the berries.

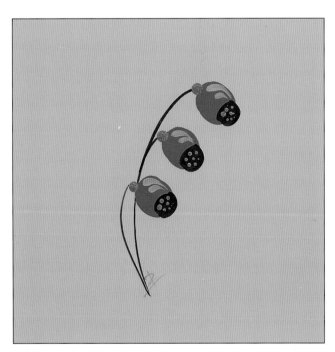

4 Place a dot of Glorious Gold at the bases of each of the berries after the stems have been painted. Place smaller dots of Glorious Gold in the Deep Midnight Blue ovals.

Painting Roses With Deanne Fortnam

Antiquing

After the design is completed and the paint has had a day or so to cure, you can antique the clock if you wish. Wear protective gloves and work in a well-ventilated room. Load some Blending and Glazing Medium on a lint-free rag or paper towel and lightly coat the entire front surface of the painted clock board. With a palette knife, mix equal parts of Raw Umber and Burnt Umber oil paint. (You don't need very much of this mix.) Using the same cloth as before, pick up some of the oil paint mix and lightly coat the painted surface. (This is the scary part! You may want to try this on a practice piece first so you can get a feel for how this works.) Use a clean, dry cloth and, starting from the center and working outward, wipe up the excess paint, leaving the antiquing heavier on the edges of the clock board. You can antique as light or as dark as you wish. I didn't antique the center of the clock face because I wanted to leave that as the lightest value area. Make sure to also antique the gold edges of the clock board.

The first time I wanted to antique over a painting, it took me a week to get enough courage to put that dark oil paint over my work. I still prefer not to antique very heavily. Many people like it a lot darker than I do and that's perfectly OK. Do try the antiquing, however scary it seems, because it can really give your work a lovely, soft, aged patina that can't be achieved otherwise.

You can rub off as much or as little of the antiquing glaze as you wish. I prefer to keep my antiquing light.

Finishing

When you are finished with the antiquing, place your clock in as dust-free an environment as you can find and let it dry for a week or so. I like to give the piece a light spray of Krylon Matte #1311 before varnishing. I didn't put any finish over the painting on the clock face under the bezel as it will be protected by the glass. When the surface is dry, assemble the clock and get ready to listen to your friends' compliments when they see what you have made!

Pattern for clock

This pattern may be hand-traced or photocopied for personal use only. Enlarge at 181% to return the image to full size.

Detail of clock

Norwegian Trunk

This lovely, small trunk is the perfect place to tuck away your special treasures. It would be wonderful as a jewelry box or would make a fantastic wedding present for a bride to store her wedding keepsakes. If you decide to paint the trunk for a wedding or anniversary present, you could omit the narrow design on the front of the lid and paint the names of the couple and their wedding date in its place.

This piece is painted in the Rogaland style of Rosemaling, which is my personal favorite of the many styles of Norwegian folk art. Rogaland painting is characterized by symmetrical designs that are precisely painted, with distinct contrasts in value and color. This is an intermediate-level project that will require good skills with side loading and especially with line and strokework. You will notice that the strokes on this piece are Norwegian teardrops instead of the regular comma strokes. Teardrop strokes are pulled from the tail to the head instead of head to tail as in the commas. You can review their execution on page 19.

Don't let the amount of painting on this piece discourage you from trying it. This is a wonderful project for improving your technical skills. If you ordinarily don't like to paint stroke pieces because you don't feel your skill level is good enough, I recommend you paint *many* stroke pieces. Only through much repetition will your technical skills improve. Learning the brush control required to paint this type of piece will help to improve the quality and ease of execution of all your paintings. If you feel that the whole trunk is too large for you to tackle, use one of the smaller designs from the sides of the trunk to decorate a smaller piece. Remember to practice your strokes before painting on the piece to achieve better brush control. Once you see how easy it is to paint this design following the step-by-step illustrations, I know you will be inspired to try your hand at the larger composition.

Materials

Palette

DecoArt Americana acrylic paints

- Antique Green
- Black Green
- Brilliant Red
- Burnt Sienna
- Charcoal Grey
- Dove Grey
- Driftwood
- Graphite
- Jade Green
- Light Buttermilk
- Olde Gold
- Primary Yellow (Cadmium Yellow Deep)
- Raw Umber
- Titanium (Snow) White
- Williamsburg Blue
- Yellow Ochre

Surface

This small wooden trunk can be purchased from Covered Bridge Crafts, 449 Amherst Street, Nashua, NH 03063. (800) 405-4464.

Brushes

To paint this project, you will need a large flat for basecoating the piece, a no. 4 through no. 14 flats, a Winsor & Newton series 12, no. 4 for stippling, a no. 00 script liner and a Winsor & Newton series 7, no. 2 for the Norwegian teardrop strokes.

I detailed the inside of the trunk using some of the elements from the outside, in a coordinating blue.

Preparation

Fill all the nail holes with wood filler, allow them to dry and then sand the filler smooth. Next, seal and sand the trunk inside and out. Now basecoat the outside of the trunk and the narrow inner lip of the base and lid with Graphite. You'll basecoat the inside of the trunk later. When this is dry, you can transfer the pattern.

Painting Procedure

Set up your palette as described on page 13 with the following value scales. Place each color family from dark to light in a separate area of your palette. The individual palette lists and step-by-step instructions will use the value scale names given in the left column below, rather than the names of the bottled colors or mixtures of colors. For example, when the instructions call for Dark Green, you simply find the darkest green on your palette, rather than checking the colors laid out on your palette against the bottle names to determine which one is Black Green.

Scalloped Edges

Paint the scalloped edges around the perimeter of the trunk with the Medium Blue mix. Side load a no. 12 flat and highlight toward the inside of each section with the Light Blue mix. Shade against the outside edges with side loads of the Dark Blue color on a no. 12 flat.

Major Elements

Many of the design elements in this pattern overlap and are easier to execute if you paint them from the bottom up. For that reason, I recommend you paint the scrolls first, the leaves next and the large blossoms last. The small blossoms half-hidden under the leaves on the front of the trunk should be painted before the leaves that overlap them. The red roses can be painted at any time while you are working on the major design elements.

Line Work

Paint the cross-hatching after the major design elements are completed. Use your script liner with thinned Medium Blue mix. When painting the cross-hatching, try to keep all the lines evenly spaced and all the same width. This will give a more polished look to your finished piece. Paint the lines on the leaves with the Light Green mix. Paint the remainder of the line work with thinned Dark Gray mix. If you are unsure of your skills at pulling long lines, I recommend that you slip your pattern under a sheet of waxed palette paper and practice pulling the line work before you paint it on the trunk. The best way to paint flowing line work is to paint it without using a pattern line. Your line work can look very stiff if you are rigidly following a pattern. If you must follow a pattern line, make sure to lighten your graphite lines until they are barely visible. If you leave any graphite showing under the painted line, you won't be able to remove it.

Teardrop Strokes

The Norwegian teardrop strokes are pulled after the lines are finished. Load the series 7, no. 2 sable brush first with Medium Gray for the head of the stroke and then with the Dark Gray mix for the tail. Pull the strokes from the tail, sitting the brush down to form the head, as shown on page 19.

LIGHT BLUE	2½ parts Dove Grey + 1 part Graphite + 1 part Williamsburg Blue
MEDIUM BLUE	1 part Graphite + 1 part Williamsburg Blue
DARK BLUE	Graphite
LIGHT GREEN	1 part Jade Green + 1 part Olde Gold
MEDIUM GREEN	Antique Green
DARK GREEN	Black Green
LIGHT GRAY	2 parts Titanium White + 1 part Driftwood
MEDIUM GRAY	Driftwood
DARK GRAY	1 part Driftwood + 1 part Raw Umber
VERY DARK GRAY	Raw Umber
LIGHT RED	2 parts Primary Yellow + 1 part Brilliant Red
MEDIUM RED	2 parts Burnt Sienna + 1 part Brilliant Red
DARK RED	2 parts Charcoal Grey + 1 part Brilliant Red

Painting Roses With Deanne Fortnam

SCROLLS

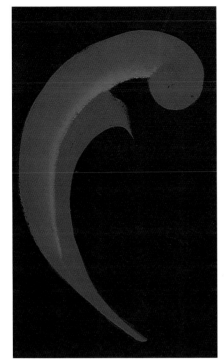
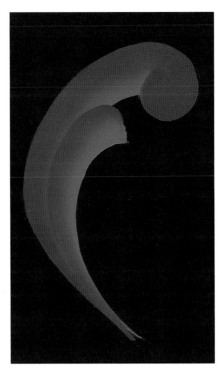
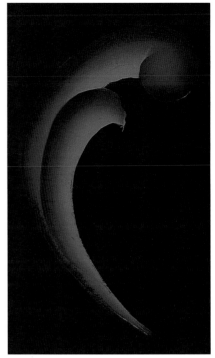

1 Basecoat the scrolls with the Medium Blue mix. Side load a no. 12 or no. 14 flat brush with the Light Blue mix and highlight the inside of the large outer scroll. Start at the curled upper head of the scroll and bring the brush down to a chisel edge against the inside scroll.

2 Side load a no. 12 or no. 14 flat with the Light Blue mix and highlight the inside edge of the inner scroll.

3 Side load a no. 14 flat with Dark Blue and shade against the outside edges of the scrolls. You may lose the outside edge of the large outer scroll because this is the same color as the background. If this happens, you may need to put the pattern line back on before proceeding to step 4.

Palette
- Light Blue mix
- Medium Blue mix
- Dark Blue
- Dark Green

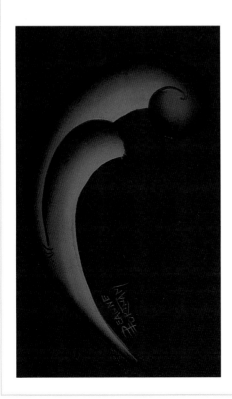

4 Side load a no. 10 flat with Dark Green and reinforce the shading against the outside edges of the scrolls. With your script liner, pull a line of Dark Green against the outside edges and around the heads of the scrolls.

LEAVES

Palette
- Light Green mix
- Medium Green
- Dark Green

1 Basecoat the leaves with Medium Green. Double load a flat brush with Medium Green and Dark Green, using a no. 12 for the large leaves and a no. 10 for the smaller leaves. Shade against the back sides of the leaves (the long sides that are not notched) with this double-loaded brush.

2 Side load a flat brush with a mixture of 1 part Light Green mix + 1 part Medium Green, using a no. 14 for the larger leaves and a no. 12 for the smaller leaves. Highlight the notched edges of the leaves.

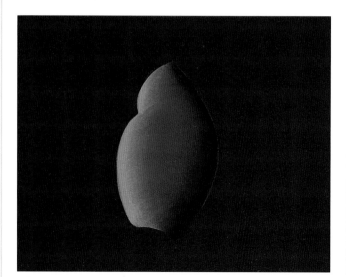

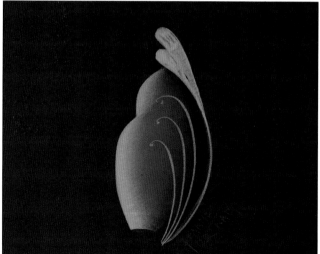

3 Reinforce the highlights with a smaller flat brush (no. 10 for the larger leaves and a no. 8 for the smaller leaves) side loaded with the Light Green mix.

4 Use your script liner brush loaded with thinned Light Green mix to pull the lines on the leaves. These lines should be pulled starting at the base of the leaf and following the shape of the outside edge. Pull teardrop strokes from the base to the tip of the leaves with your series 7, no. 2 sable brush loaded with Light Green mix.

BLOSSOMS

Palette
- Light Gray mix
- Medium Gray
- Dark Gray mix
- Very Dark Gray
- Light Red mix
- Medium Red mix
- Dark Red mix
- Dark Green
- Titanium White
- Yellow Ochre
- Primary Yellow

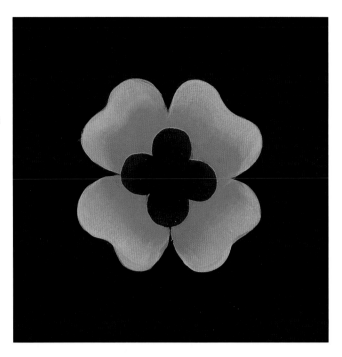

1 Basecoat the outer petals with Medium Gray. Side load a no. 14 flat with the Light Gray mix and highlight the outside edges of the petals. Basecoat the small, inner petals with the Medium Red mix. Side load a no. 10 flat with the Dark Red mix and shade against the inside edge of the centers.

2 Side load a no. 12 flat with Titanium White and reinforce the highlights against the outside edges of the petals. Side load a no. 6 flat with Dark Green. Reinforce the shading on the small, inner petals against the center.

3 Side load a no. 14 flat with the Dark Gray mix. Shade the inside of the large petals against the red inner petals. Side load a no. 6 flat with the Dark Gray mix and shade against the turned edges. Side load a no. 10 flat with Light Red mix and highlight the outside edges of the red petals.

4 Side load a no. 10 flat with Very Dark Gray. Reinforce the shading on the large petals against the red inner petals. Side load a no. 4 flat with the same color and reinforce the shading against the turned edges. Basecoat the blossom centers with Yellow Ochre. Shade around the outside edges of the centers with a no. 10 flat side loaded with a mixture of 1 part Very Dark Gray + 1 part Yellow Ochre. Next, reinforce the shading with a no. 6 flat side loaded with Very Dark Gray.

5 With your script liner, pull a line of Very Dark Gray against the turned edges of the large petals. Pull embellishing lines of a mixture of 1 part Very Dark Gray + 1 part Dark Gray mix on the large outer petals. Make sure to follow the shape of the outer petal edges when pulling these lines. Begin highlighting the flower centers by stippling on Primary Yellow. Use the Winsor & Newton series 12, no. 4 to create the stippling. Start at the middle of the centers and work until you slightly overlap the shading. Reinforce the highlighting in the very center by stippling on Titanium White.

6 Load the Winsor & Newton series 7, no. 2 brush with Medium Gray, then Very Dark Gray on the tip of the brush. Paint a series of three small teardrops where the red inner petals join. Place a brush handle dot of the Light Gray mix at the tips of the teardrops, against the flower centers.

ROSES

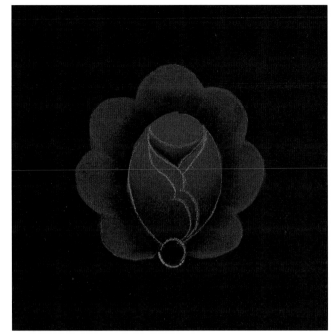

1 Basecoat the roses with the Medium Red mix. Side load a no. 14 flat with the Dark Red mix and shade against the bottoms of the center ovals of the roses. On the large roses, shade the outside petals against the inner ovals. (You will need to use a smaller flat to shade the outside petals of the smaller roses on the sides of the trunk.) Side load a no. 6 flat with the Dark Red mix and shade the throat of the roses.

2 Side load a no. 10 flat with Dark Green and reinforce the shading on the outside petals against the center ovals of the roses. (Again, you will need to use a smaller brush for the smaller roses on the sides of the trunk.)

Palette

- Light Red mix
- Medium Red mix
- Dark Red mix
- Light Gray mix
- Medium Gray
- Dark Gray mix
- Very Dark Gray
- Dark Green
- Titanium White
- Yellow Ochre
- Primary Yellow

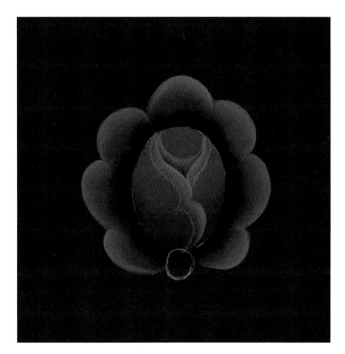

3 Side load a no. 10 to no. 12 flat with the Light Red mix and highlight the outside edges of the outer petals. Side load a no. 8 flat with the Light Red mix and create the highlights in the centers of the roses as shown.

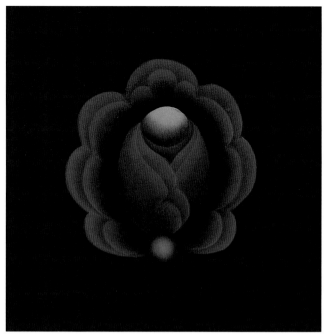

4 Side load a no. 10 flat with the Light Red mix and paint the inner row of highlights on the outer petals and in the center ovals.

5 Basecoat the rose centers with Yellow Ochre. Shade the centers with a no. 10 flat side loaded with a mixture of 1 part Very Dark Gray + 1 part Yellow Ochre. Reinforce the shading with a no. 6 flat side loaded with Very Dark Gray. Basecoat the circle at the bases of the roses with Medium Gray. Side load a no. 6 flat with the Dark Gray mix and shade around the outside edges of the circles. Reinforce the shading with a no. 4 flat side loaded with Very Dark Gray.

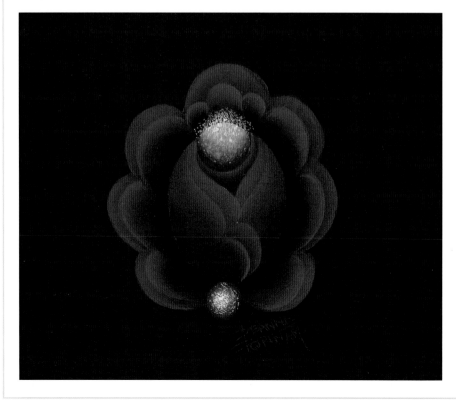

6 Highlight the yellow centers of the roses by stippling on Primary Yellow, then Titanium White. Highlight the center of the circles by stippling on the Light Gray mix, then Titanium White.

Finishing

Basecoat the inside of the trunk and the tray with Light Buttermilk. It will take several coats of this light value to cover opaquely, so make sure you don't leave any of the wood showing through. I recommend you wait to paint the inside of the trunk until after you've finished all the decorative painting on the outside. It's easy to get dirty fingerprints on the light color when you are working on painting the design.

Pattern for sides of trunk

This pattern may be hand-traced or photocopied for personal use only. Enlarge at 114% to return the image to full size.

Detail of side of trunk

Pattern for top of lid

This pattern may be hand-traced or photocopied for personal use only. Enlarge at 156% to return the image to full size.

Detail of top of lid

Painting Roses With Deanne Fortnam

Pattern for front of trunk

This pattern may be hand-traced or photocopied for personal use only. Enlarge at 128% to return the image to full size.

Russian Box

I have greatly admired the numerous, beautiful styles of Russian folk art painting for many years. My personal favorite is the richly elegant Zhostovo style, characterized by exquisite flowers painted with brilliant colors and dynamic value contrasts. These graceful designs seem to glow with a life of their own.

Zhostovo designs are ordinarily painted in oils. The techniques for achieving this look in acrylics are dramatically different from the traditional oil methods. I think the end result, regardless of the process, still has the look of its Russian inspiration.

This style is very loose and free-flowing with a lot of overstroking and line work. The beginnings of each flower form will be basecoated with side-loaded shading as you have done on previous projects. The highlighting will be drybrushed with a sable round, which will be a new technique. As I recommend with anything new, you should practice first and become comfortable with the dry-brushed highlights before you paint on your wood piece. I highly recommend using the Yarka sable brushes for this process, because it will be easier to achieve the loosely stroked highlights.

Although this piece looks complicated, it is based on the building blocks of the techniques you have already learned. Completing it will help you master better brush handling, and the borders will certainly improve your technical skills. You don't have to paint the complex border shown on my box—use only part of the border or create one of your own.

I hope you will give this project a try. I know you will enjoy working with the brilliant palette and learning something new.

Preparation

Seal and sand the box inside and out. Now basecoat the outside of the box and lid with Black Green and the inside of the box and lid with True Red or the color of your choice. The insides of Russian boxes are traditionally painted red. When the paint is dry, you can transfer the pattern.

Painting Procedure

Set up a palette as described on page 13 with the following value scales. The individual palettes and step-by-step instructions will use the value names in the left column, rather than the bottle names or mixes.

Work from the bottom to the top design elements. Paint the leaves first, then the berries, the blue flowers, the white filler flowers and last the roses and buds. Traditionally the roses and main design elements would be painted first, then all the supportive elements added, but because you aren't designing this piece freehand, you will find it easier to work as I have recommended above.

Materials

Palette

DecoArt Americana acrylic paints
- Alizarin Crimson
- Black Green
- Blue Violet
- Blush Flesh
- Boysenberry Pink
- Charcoal Grey
- Cranberry Wine
- Glorious Gold (Dazzling Metallics)
- Hauser Dark Green
- Hauser Medium Green
- Light Buttermilk
- Napa Red
- Raw Sienna
- Shale Green
- Spice Pink
- True Red
- Yellow Light

Surface

This 10¾"-diameter (27.3cm) octagonal box is available from Covered Bridge Crafts, 449 Amherst Street, Nashua, NH 03063. (800) 405-4464.

Brushes

To paint this project, you will need a large flat brush for basecoating the box, no. 6 through no. 14 flats, a no. 4 liner, no. 3 and no. 4 Yarka Kolinsky sable rounds and a good script liner. You may also find it helpful to have a Winsor & Newton series 12, no. 4 miniature sable for basecoating the flower forms.

Miscellaneous

It would be helpful to have an inexpensive compass to mark the guideline for placing the stroke borders.

Roses and Rosebuds

The roses are basecoated petal by petal. I have indicated on the pattern on page 76 which value is to be painted on each petal. It is important to get these values correct to create the flow of value from the light to the dark sides of the roses.

The shading is side loaded, but the highlights are drybrushed using shape-following sable brush strokes. Paint the highlights one petal at a time. You will notice that the brush marks are left showing. In the illustrations you can see where the rounded end of the brush is set down. Use very light pressure as you pull the brush, just skimming the surface, then lifting it off. If you wish to create a slightly smoother stroke, lightly dampen the surface of the petal before you pull the highlight. You will also need to thin the paint a bit so that it pulls evenly from the tips of the bristles. Experiment on a piece of scrap paper until you get the feel.

The line work on the roses should be pulled in a loose and free manner, accenting the outside edges of the petals.

I have included one step-by-step rosebud to show you the process. Paint the other buds in the same manner,

PINK 1	1 part Spice Pink + 2 parts Light Buttermilk
PINK 2	1 part Spice Pink + 1 part Light Buttermilk
PINK 3	Spice Pink
PINK 4	3 parts Alizarin Crimson + 1 part Spice Pink
PINK 5	3 parts Alizarin Crimson + 1 part Boysenberry Pink
PINK 6	1½ parts Cranberry Wine + 1 part Boysenberry Pink + 1 part Alizarin Crimson
PINK 7	1 part Alizarin Crimson + 1 part Napa Red
RED 1	1 part Red 2 + 1 part Light Buttermilk
RED 2	1½ parts Red 3 + 1 part Light Buttermilk
RED 3	1 part True Red + 1 part Blush Flesh
RED 4	1 part True Red + a touch of Yellow Light
RED 5	1 part True Red + a touch of Black Green
RED 6	5 parts True Red + 1 part Black Green
RED 7	3 parts True Red + 1 part Black Green

varying them a little bit as shown in the detail photos.

Leaves

I have given you three different colors of leaves in the illustration. The inner, lighter leaves should be the warmest and brightest. As you move to the outer edges of the design, the color should be cooled and dulled a bit. I basecoated all my leaves by brush mixing the colors. No two are exactly the same. I began with Hauser Medium Green and brush mixed a little

Charcoal Grey to get the duller colors. The cooler leaves at the outer edges of the design have some Hauser Dark Green mixed into the Hauser Medium Green and Charcoal Grey. Pick up the medium value pink mixes to accent the leaves, and in a few places use some of the blue mixes from your palette.

The additional line work that accents the piece is painted with a liner brush and a mix of either a medium pink or red from the palette plus some Charcoal Grey, or Hauser Medium Green plus some Charcoal Grey.

Border for bottom of box

Painting Roses With Deanne Fortnam

The lightest value areas should be where the two roses join and the light values should fade away from this central area.

Borders

You can paint the gold borders either before or after the painting is completed. I used a no. 4 liner for the strokes and a good script liner for the line work. All of the border work was painted with Glorious Gold. Mark a guide line ⅛" (0.3cm) from the bottom of the box with your compass and use this to position the first line of strokes. The strokes that begin the border on the box lid are placed just above the corner formed from the routed edge. Both of the borders begin with a line of basic S-strokes, shown on page 18.

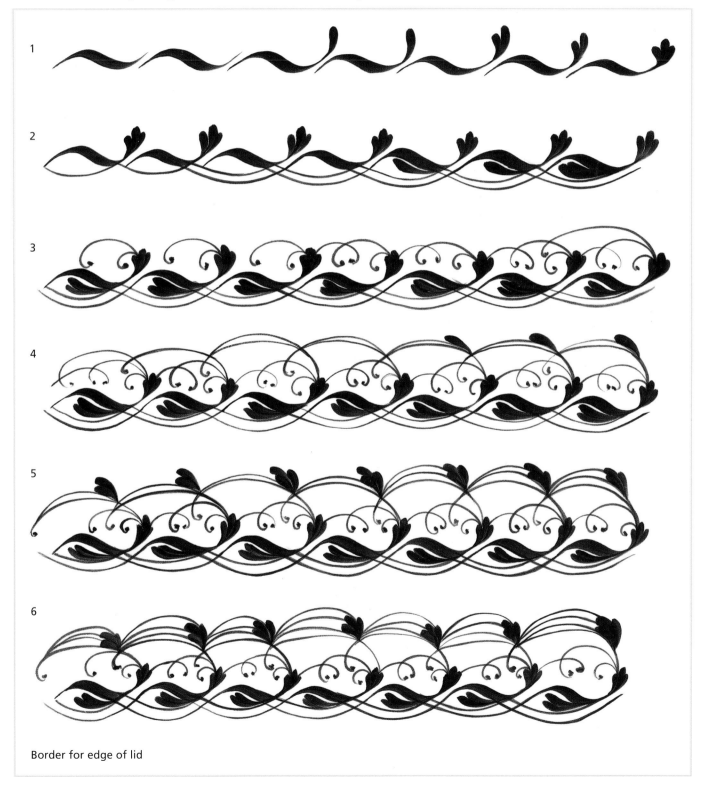

Border for edge of lid

LEAVES

Palette
- Hauser Medium Green
- Charcoal Grey
- Hauser Dark Green
- Black Green
- Light Buttermilk
- a medium value pink
- Blue Violet

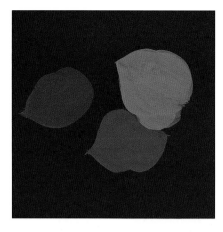

1 Basecoat the leaves working one leaf color at a time. The different colors are achieved by brush mixing the paints. The lighter, brighter leaves are toward the center of the design and the cooler leaves toward the outer edges of the design. Basecoat the lightest leaves with Hauser Medium Green, the middle leaves with Hauser Medium Green + Charcoal Grey and the darkest leaves with Hauser Medium Green + Charcoal Grey + Hauser Dark Green.

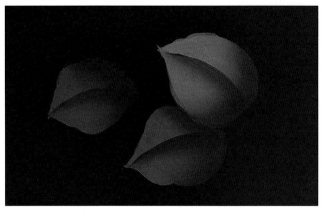

2 Side load a large flat with Black Green. Shade the bases of the leaves and against one side of the center veins.

3 Brush mix the leaf color with Light Buttermilk to lighten the value. Using a no. 4 Yarka sable, pick up the highlight color and thin with a small amount of water. Blot excess water off the brush, then lightly stroke the highlights, using shape-following strokes that fade away as you lift the brush.

4 Lighten the first highlight color with more Light Buttermilk and overstroke the highlights one more time, keeping the lighter value in a smaller area.

5 Side load a medium value pink on a no. 10 flat and accent the tips of the leaves. The blue accents can be side loaded with a mix of Blue Violet plus a small amount of Light Buttermilk.

Load a script liner with the basecoat color plus Light Buttermilk and pull the center veins, some side veins and the outer, flowing accenting lines.

BERRIES

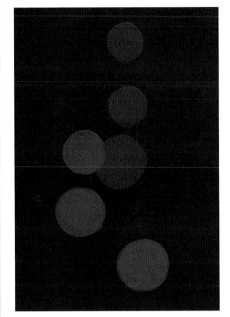

1 Basecoat the berries using the red value scale as indicated on the pattern.

2 Side load Red 4 on a no. 8 flat and paint a reflected light on the shadow side of the berries.

3 Side load Red 3 on a no. 10 flat and highlight the berries.

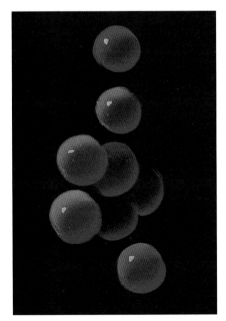

Palette

- Reds 1 through 7
- Light Buttermilk
- Black Green
- Blue Violet
- Hauser Medium Green
- Charcoal Grey

4 Side load Red 2 on a no. 8 flat and reinforce the highlights on the berries. Next, using a no. 6 flat, side load Red 1 and reinforce the highlights on the lightest value berries. Place a high shine with the tip of a liner brush using Red 1 mixed with a small amount of Light Buttermilk.

5 Paint a blossom end with the tip of a round or liner brush loaded with Black Green. Accent a few of the berries with a side load of Blue Violet plus a small amount of Light Buttermilk. Paint the stems with a liner brush loaded with Hauser Medium Green plus a small amount of Charcoal Grey. The highlights are painted with the above mix, lightened with a small amount of Light Buttermilk.

BLUE FLOWERS

1 Basecoat the flowers with a mix of 2 parts Blue Violet + 1 part Light Buttermilk. Lighten this mix with more Light Buttermilk and side load a highlight in the center of the flower using a no. 14 flat.

2 Side load a no. 10 flat with Blue Violet and shade between the flower petals, some outside edges and in the flower centers. Make sure some of the center highlight extends beyond the shading.

3 Brush mix some Black Green plus Blue Violet and use this mix to reinforce the shading. Use a no. 8 flat to side load this step. After the shading is dry, dampen the flowers, then using a no. 8 flat side loaded with the above mix, pull some lines from the centers about one-third of the way into the flower petals.

4 Make a light blue mix with Light Buttermilk plus some Blue Violet. Use a no. 3 Yarka sable to drybrush highlights on the flower petals.

5 Lighten the highlight mix with more Light Buttermilk and reinforce the highlights in a few places. Pull accent lines around flower petals with Light Buttermilk plus Blue Violet on a liner brush. Side load accents of Pink 4 on a no. 10 flat. Place a dot of Raw Sienna in the centers of the flowers using the tip of a liner brush. When this is dry, place a smaller dot on each of the Raw Sienna dots with Yellow Light.

Palette
- Blue Violet
- Light Buttermilk
- Black Green
- Pink 4
- Raw Sienna
- Yellow Light

Painting Roses With Deanne Fortnam

WHITE FLOWERS

1 Stroke in a basecoat of Shale Green using a Winsor & Newton series 12, no. 4.

2 Shade the flowers with a no. 10 flat side loaded with Black Green.

3 Drybrush highlights with Shale Green plus Light Buttermilk with a no. 3 Yarka sable.

4 Reinforce some of the highlights with Light Buttermilk. These will also be drybrushed with the no. 3 Yarka sable. Pull accent lines of Light Buttermilk plus a small amount of Shale Green.

Palette
- Shale Green
- Black Green
- Light Buttermilk
- Pink 4
- Blue Violet
- Yellow Light
- Hauser Medium Green
- Charcoal Grey

5 Side load accents of Pink 4 with a no. 8 flat. Side load a no. 8 flat with Blue Violet and paint a C-stroke to create the flower centers. Paint dots of Blue Violet around the centers with the tip of a liner brush. Place a dot of Yellow Light in the center of each flower. Paint the stems using a liner brush with Hauser Medium Green plus Charcoal Grey. Paint a few highlight lines with the liner brush and the above mix, lightened with Light Buttermilk.

R O S E B U D S

Palette

- Pinks 1 through 7
- Hauser Medium Green
- Charcoal Grey
- Light Buttermilk

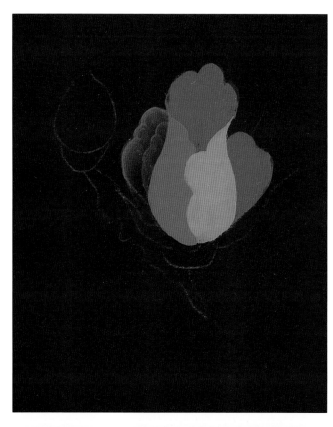

1 Side load the transparent petals with a no. 10 flat side loaded with Pink 4. Basecoat the buds using the pink value scale, as indicated on the pattern on page 76.

2 Shade the buds with a no. 10 flat side loaded with Pink 7.

3 Using a no. 8 flat, highlight the dark sections with side loads of Pink 3 and the light sections with side loads of Pink 2.

Painting Roses With Deanne Fortnam

4 Reinforce the highlights on the front of the buds by drybrushing Pink 1 using a no. 3 or no. 4 Yarka sable. Pull accent lines, outlining the petal edges, with Pink 1.

5 Basecoat the calyxes, green buds and stems with a mix of Hauser Medium Green plus Charcoal Grey.

6 Lighten the green basecoat with Light Buttermilk and drybrush highlights using a no. 3 Yarka sable. Pull highlight lines and accent dots using a liner brush and the basecoat green plus Light Buttermilk.

ROSES

Palette

- Pinks 1 through 7
- Reds 1 through 7
- Black Green
- Light Buttermilk
- Raw Sienna
- Yellow Light
- Blue Violet

1 The red and pink roses are painted in the same manner. Use the pink value scale for the larger pink rose and the red value scale for the smaller red rose. The larger pink rose is illustrated. Side load a no. 12 flat with Pink 4 and paint the outer, transparent petals.

2 Basecoat as indicated on the pattern on page 76.

3 Use a flat brush appropriate to the size of the area you are working to shade the petals. The large outer petals will require a no. 14 flat and the smaller petals a no. 10. Shade the petals basecoated with Pink 2 and Pink 3 with side loads of Pink 5. Shade the remainder of the large outer petals with Pink 7. Shade the innermost petal in the throat of the rose with a side load of Pink 7 using a no. 12 flat. Reinforce the shading on the three darkest, outer petals on the right of the rose with a side load of Pink 7 plus a small amount of Black Green, using a no. 12 flat. Basecoat the turned-back edges on the petals with Pink 5 on the light petals and Pink 3 on the dark petals.

Painting Roses With Deanne Fortnam

4 Begin drybrushing the highlights on the petals with a no. 4 Yarka sable. Begin by using one value lighter than the basecoat on each of the petals, making sure to follow the shape and direction of the petals. Go up two values from the basecoat and reinforce the highlights. The petals that were basecoated with Pink 2 will have Light Buttermilk for the final highlight.

5 Accent the outer petal edges with line work using Pink 1. Paint dots of Raw Sienna and then Yellow Light in the throats of the roses. Side load blue accents on a few of the outer petals with a mix of 2 parts Blue Violet + 1 part Light Buttermilk.

Pattern for Russian box

Painting Roses With Deanne Fortnam

Detail of lid

Detail of border on bottom of box

Yellow Roses and Violets

This small, canvas-covered jewelry box would come in handy to tuck away your favorite treasures. The roses on this project are a little more advanced than those in project 4. Although they still begin with a simple oval, the side petals on this project begin outside and then overlap the center oval. This project builds on the skills you've gained by painting the previous projects. You'll be using a double-loaded angle brush to pull the rose petals and to paint the violets, and you'll also need good side-loading skills to add the extra highlights, shadows and accents.

For this project I used a soft, blended background that harmonizes with the colors in the design. This is currently one of my favorite background treatments because you can begin with a neutral value, pick up colors from the design elements and then wet-on-wet blend them into the basecoat. Experiment with your favorite designs and create your own unique backgrounds.

Materials

Palette
DecoArt Americana acrylic paints
- Antique Green
- Black Plum
- Golden Straw
- Jade Green
- Light Avocado
- Light Buttermilk
- Lilac
- Pineapple
- Plantation Pine
- Primary Red
- Primary Yellow
- Raw Sienna
- Reindeer Moss Green
- Royal Purple

Surface
This small, canvas-covered jewelry box can be purchased from Dalee Bookbinding Co./Creations in Canvas, 129 Clinton Place, Yonkers, NY 10701. (914) 965-1660.

Brushes
To paint this project, you will need a large flat for basecoating the piece; a Loew-Cornell series 7600, ¾-inch (19mm) filbert mop to create the blended background; no. 8, no. 10, no. 12, ⅜-inch (10mm) and ¾-inch (19mm) flats; ¼-inch (6mm) and ⅜-inch (10mm) angle brushes; a no. 2 round and a good script liner.

Preparation

Basecoat the lid of the box with Light Buttermilk. Basecoat the sides, back and bottom of the box with Shale Green. The lower lip on the box can be painted with Light Avocado.

When the lid is dry, dampen the surface with clean water and then basecoat it again with Light Buttermilk thinned with water. While this is still wet, pick up Plantation Pine with the ¾-inch (19mm) filbert mop and blend into the wet background, working from the lower right corner toward the upper left. Use a slip-slap motion of the brush to blend the colors together. You will need to reinforce the Plantation Pine several times. Each time you pick up more of the Plantation Pine, blend from the lower right toward the upper left. When you have worked in enough green, wipe the brush and pick up Medium Purple (Royal Purple). Blend this randomly into the wet background. As this color starts to dry, you will begin to see drybrush marks in the background. This is fine as it adds texture to the background. Try to keep the upper left corner of the background lighter than the lower right.

Painting Procedure

Set up your palette as described on page 13, with the value scales given on this page. The individual palettes and step-by-step instructions will use the value names listed in the left column, rather than the bottle names or mixes. Start with the violets under the leaves first. Next paint the leaves, the violets that are on top of the leaves and then the roses.

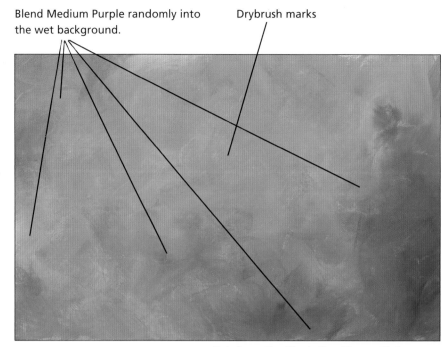

Blend Medium Purple randomly into the wet background.

Drybrush marks

Reinforce the Plantation Pine until the lower right corner is as dark as shown.

Roses

The double-loaded petal strokes on the roses are a little tricky at first, but if you practice, you will eventually be able to pull them effortlessly. Begin with the petals at the bottom of the roses, overlapping as you work toward the uppermost petals. Load the angle brush with the light value on the longer bristles and the dark value on the shorter bristles. Place the brush with the light value facing the top of the rose, then swing the brush around, bringing it to a chisel edge as you pull it across the oval body of the rose. If you want to create more rippled flower petals, apply then release pressure on the brush.

Leaves

I have included warm and cool leaves in this design to help create more visual interest. The cool leaves are generally behind other design elements, and the warm leaves are on top of the cool leaves. By using the same light and dark values on both warm and cool leaves, you help to marry the two different temperature leaves together and create harmony in the design. Notice that the violet and yellow accents on the leaves help complement the major design elements and carry the colors through the design.

LIGHT PURPLE	Lilac
MEDIUM PURPLE	Royal Purple
DARK PURPLE	1 part Royal Purple + 1 part Black Plum
LIGHT YELLOW	Pineapple
MEDIUM YELLOW	Golden Straw
DARK YELLOW	2 parts Raw Sienna + 1 part Black Plum

Painting Roses With Deanne Fortnam

VIOLETS

1 Double load a ⅜-inch (10mm) angle brush with Light Purple and Medium Purple and pull the two upper petals on each of the violets. Double load a ⅜-inch (10mm) angle brush with Light Buttermilk and Medium Purple and pull the remaining violet petals.

2 Side load a no. 10 flat with the Dark Purple mix and shade against the outside edges of the violet petals. With this same side load, shade against the flower centers of the two upper petals on each violet.

3 Pull vein lines of the Dark Purple mix from the center out with a good script liner. Pull the veins about half to two-thirds of the way to the outside edge.

4 Place a sit-down of Medium Yellow in the center of the violets with a no. 2 round or any small round brush.

5 Shade against the right side of the Medium Yellow sit-down with a very small side load of Primary Red. Create a very thin side load of Primary Yellow on a no. 10 flat. Use this to subtly accent a few of the violet petals.

Palette
- Light Purple
- Medium Purple
- Dark Purple mix
- Light Buttermilk
- Medium Yellow
- Primary Red
- Primary Yellow

LEAVES

Palette
- Antique Green
- Light Avocado
- Reindeer Moss Green
- Jade Green
- Plantation Pine
- Black Plum
- Medium Purple
- Light Buttermilk

1 Basecoat the leaves marked AG on the pattern on page 85 with Antique Green and the leaves marked LA with Light Avocado.

2 Brush mix some Reindeer Moss Green plus Antique Green. Side load a no. 12 flat with this mix and highlight the Antique Green leaves. Side load a no. 12 flat with Jade Green and highlight the Light Avocado leaves.

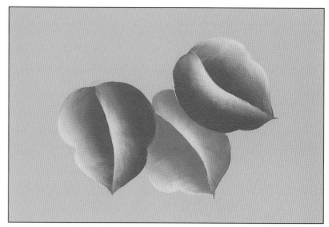

3 Reinforce the highlights on all the leaves with a no. 8 flat side loaded with Reindeer Moss Green.

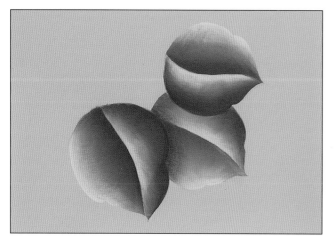

4 Shade all the leaves with a no. 12 flat side loaded with Plantation Pine.

5 Accent the tips of the leaves with side loads of Black Plum and a mixture of Medium Purple plus a little Light Buttermilk. Using thinned Reindeer Moss Green, pull the vein lines on the leaves. Pull the center vein first, keeping it on the shadow color, then the side veins. Don't pull the veins to the outside edges of the leaves.

ROSES

Palette
- Light Yellow
- Medium Yellow
- Dark Yellow mix
- Primary Yellow
- Light Buttermilk

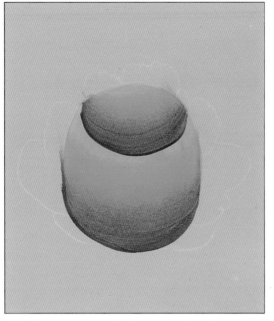

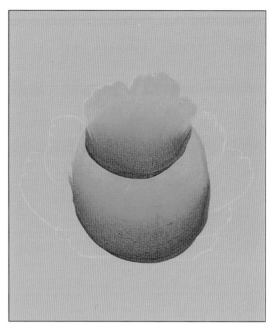

1 The roses and rosebuds are painted in the same manner, using smaller brushes when painting the buds. Basecoat the center ovals with Medium Yellow. Side load a ¾-inch (19mm) flat with the Dark Yellow mix and shade against the bases and throats of the roses.

2 Side load a no. 12 flat with Medium Yellow and paint the upper petals of the roses.

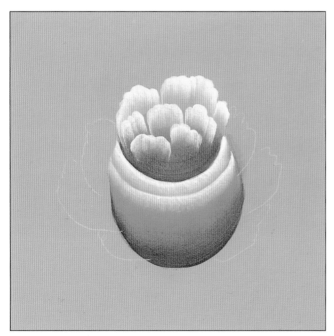

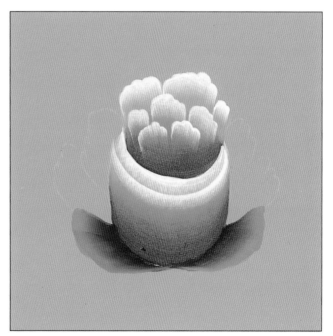

3 Side load a no. 10 flat with Light Yellow, highlight the upper petals and create the lower rows of petals in the throat of the roses. Highlight the front of the roses with side loads of Light Yellow on a no. 10 flat.

4 Double load a ⅜-inch (10mm) flat with Medium Yellow and the Dark Yellow mix and paint petals on either side of the bottoms of the ovals.

5 Double load a ⅜-inch (10mm) flat with Medium Yellow and the Dark Yellow mix and paint petal strokes overlapping the bottom strokes. Make sure to bring the brush to a chisel edge and pull this across the ovals.

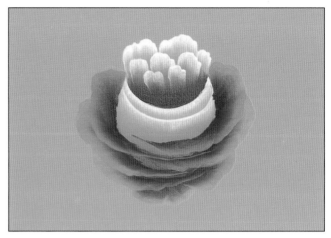

6 Pull the rest of the rose petal strokes with your ⅜-inch (10mm) flat and the same double load used in steps 4 and 5.

7 Highlight the edges of all the petals with a no. 8 flat side loaded with Light Yellow.

8 Side load Primary Yellow on a ¾-inch (19mm) flat and accent the right sides of the roses. Make sure this is a thin application of color that does not lose all the value changes on the flower petals.

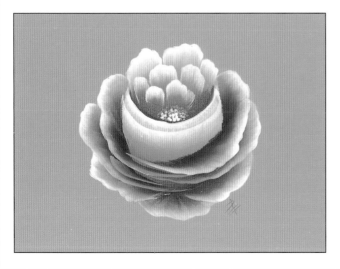

9 Highlight areas on the petal edges with a no. 8 flat side loaded with Light Buttermilk.

Painting Roses With Deanne Fortnam

Pattern for lid

Advanced Stroke Roses: Yellow Roses and Violets 85

Mauve Rose Tray

This large, wooden serving tray is a functional piece that will come in handy for so many things. I designed it to coordinate with an upholstered bench that sits in front of the sofa in my studio. The bench provides a great place to put my feet up when taking a break from work, but has no hard surface to set a drink on. This tray looks great with the fabric of the bench and the upholstery of the sofa, and gives me a serving tray as well as a place to set my coffee cup.

I've used some pearlized colors to enhance the highlight areas. I also included them in the mix for the background leaf pattern. This gives the piece a soft glimmer when the light catches the metallic paint. It is a subtle but pretty effect that I know you will enjoy working with.

You can reduce this pattern and paint it on a smaller piece to make an elegant dresser tray, or use portions of the pattern to paint coordinating pieces for your bedroom, bathroom or

wherever you want a pretty floral in these colors. You could also paint this design on a large round box, using the two or three lower roses in the design for the lid and the background leaf pattern for the sides. (Actually, that sounds pretty neat—I think I'll try it. It would make a great storage box for my bathroom!)

If the colors in your home lean more toward mauve than blue, try painting the outside of the tray with one of the values of mauve in the design instead of the blue. The tan or green would also work if that coordinates better with your colors. Don't be afraid to experiment with the colors until you find something that pleases you. Sometimes it's a hassle to try something, then decide you don't like it and have to paint it over again. Just remember, that's part of the creative process. In the long run you will be happier with your paintings if you try different things until you are pleased with the end results.

Materials

Palette
DecoArt Americana acrylic paints
- Antique Maroon
- Blue Chiffon
- Buttermilk
- Cranberry Wine
- French Grey Blue
- French Mauve
- Green Pearl (Dazzling Metallics)
- Hauser Medium Green
- Jade Green
- Khaki Tan
- Light French Blue
- Mauve
- Pink Chiffon
- Pink Satin Pearl (Dazzling Metallics)
- Raw Umber
- Sky Blue Pearl (Dazzling Metallics)
- Slate Grey
- Titanium (Snow) White
- White Pearl (Dazzling Metallics)

Surface
This 14½″ × 21½″ (36.8cm × 54.6cm) wooden tray can be purchased from Covered Bridge Crafts, 449 Amherst Street, Nashua, NH 03063. (800) 405-4464.

Brushes
To paint this project you will need a large flat for basecoating the piece; no. 4 through no. 14 flats; a 1-inch (25mm) flat; no. 4, no. 8 and no. 10 filberts; a no. 0 round; ¼-inch (6mm), ⅜-inch (10mm) and ½-inch (13mm) angle brushes; a ⅜-inch (10mm) deerfoot and a script liner.

Miscellaneous
An inexpensive compass.

Preparation

Seal and sand the entire tray inside and out. Basecoat the inside bottom of the tray with Buttermilk and the inside sides with Titanium White. Basecoat the outside of the tray with a mix of 1 part French Grey Blue + 1 part Slate Grey. Make enough of this mix to have some left over to clean up any mistakes from handling the piece while it is being painted, or wait to basecoat the outside until the painting is complete.

Transfer the red pattern lines on pages 98 and 99 with white graphite. If you can't see the white graphite on the Buttermilk background, transfer the lines with the lightest value you can see. You will be painting the background leaf design with white, which won't cover up dark graphite lines. Once you paint over the lines, you won't be able to erase them.

At this time you will need to transfer only the outside edges of the hydrangea groupings, roses, buds and leaves.

Trace the red pattern lines onto the basecoated tray. Side load a no. 14 flat brush with a mix of 2 parts Titanium White + 1 part White Pearl. With the white edge of the brush against the inside of the pattern line, pull the white around the perimeter of the leaf shape. Also pull the white edge of the brush against one side of the vein line. This will create a very subtle leaf that is brightest on the edges and vein line, and fades to the Buttermilk background in between.

Painting Procedure

Set up your palette as described on page 13 with the following value scales. The individual palettes and step-by-step instructions will use the value names listed in the left column, rather than the bottle names or mixes.

Begin this project by painting all the background leaves (indicated with the red lines on the pattern) with a no. 14 flat side loaded with a mix of 2 parts Titanium White + 1 part White Pearl.

The design elements in this piece overlap a lot, and some of the elements are stroked in. I found it easiest to work from the outside edges of each half of the design in toward the large center roses. The rosebuds can be painted at any time.

Finishing

When you finish the painting, paint a stripe line with French Grey Blue on the inside edges of the tray, ¼" (0.6cm) from the upper edge. Because this piece will be used to serve drinks, it will need a heavier, more durable finish. Apply several coats of acrylic varnish, then hand-rub the surface with steel wool. You can find instructions for striping and hand-rubbed finishes in chapter four.

VERY LIGHT MAUVE	Pink Chiffon
LIGHT MAUVE	French Mauve
MEDIUM MAUVE	Mauve
DARK MAUVE	1 part Cranberry Wine + 1 part Antique Maroon
LIGHT GREEN	4 parts Titanium White + 1½ parts Jade Green + 1 part Light French Blue
MEDIUM GREEN	1½ parts Jade Green + 1 part Light French Blue
DARK GREEN	4 parts Hauser Medium Green + 1 part French Grey Blue
LIGHT BLUE	Blue Chiffon
MEDIUM BLUE	Light French Blue
DARK BLUE	French Grey Blue
LIGHT TAN	2 parts Buttermilk + 1 part Khaki Tan
MEDIUM TAN	Khaki Tan
DARK TAN	1 part Khaki Tan + 1 part Raw Umber

Painting Roses With Deanne Fortnam

LEAVES

Palette

- Light Green mix
- Medium Green mix
- Dark Green mix
- Light Tan mix
- Medium Tan
- Dark Tan mix
- Buttermilk
- Medium Mauve
- Dark Mauve mix
- Dark Blue
- Green Pearl
- Pink Satin Pearl
- Raw Umber

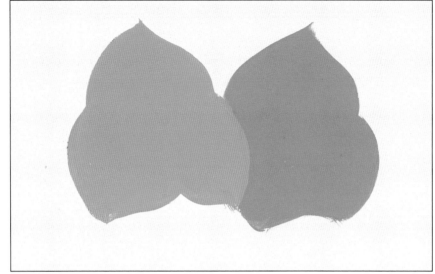

1 Basecoat the green leaves with the Medium Green mix and the tan leaves with Medium Tan.

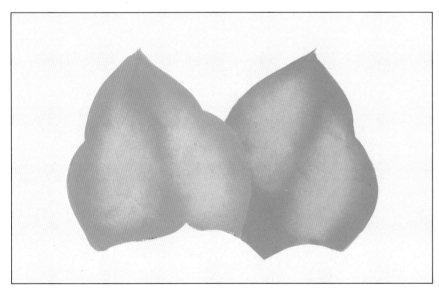

2 Paint an oval bull's eye highlight—as shown on page 15—on each side of the center veins with a side-loaded no. 10 filbert, using the Light Green mix for the green leaves and the Light Tan mix for the tan leaves.

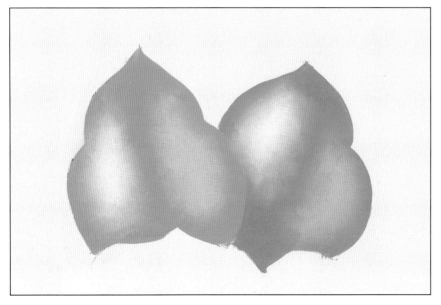

3 Reinforce one highlight on each leaf with a no. 8 filbert side loaded with Buttermilk.

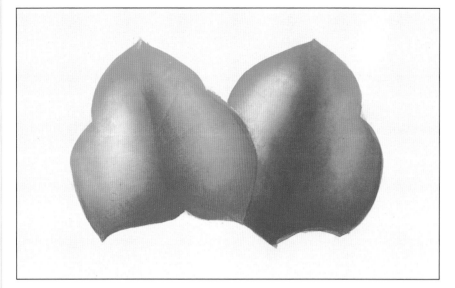

4 Side load a no. 12 flat with the Dark Green mix for the green leaves and the Dark Tan mix for the tan leaves. Shade both sides of the center veins, bringing the shading to a point as it comes into the tip of the leaves. Shade the bases of the leaves with a no. 14 flat side loaded with the Dark Green mix for the green leaves and the Dark Tan mix for the tan leaves.

5 Paint the leaf veins using a script liner loaded with thinned Medium Green mix for the green leaves and thinned Medium Tan for the tan leaves. Shade against one side of the side veins with a no. 8 flat side loaded with the Dark Green mix on the green leaves and the Dark Tan mix on the tan leaves.

6 Side load accents on the green and tan leaves with Medium Mauve, the Dark Mauve mix and Dark Blue. Brush mix some Green Pearl and Pink Satin Pearl and use this to side load shimmering accents in a few places. Reinforce the shadows on one side of the center veins and in the darkest value areas with side loads of Raw Umber on the tan leaves and a mix of Raw Umber plus the Dark Green mix on the green leaves.

HYDRANGEA

Palette
- Medium Tan
- Raw Umber
- Light Blue
- Medium Blue
- Dark Blue
- Light Mauve
- Medium Mauve
- Dark Mauve mix
- Sky Blue Pearl
- Dark Green mix

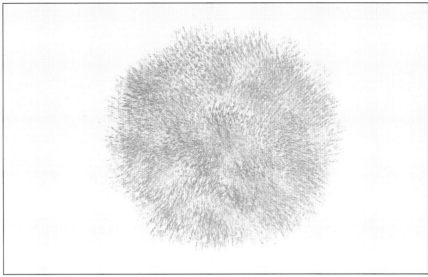

1 Use a ⅜-inch (10mm) deer-foot brush to stipple the area under the flowers with Medium Tan. Stippling is demonstrated on page 125.

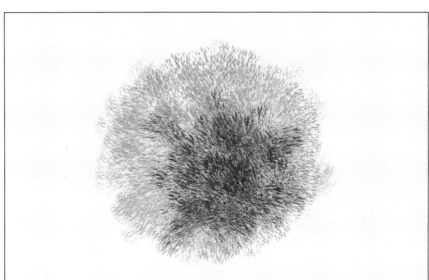

2 Using the same ⅜-inch (10mm) deerfoot, stipple with Raw Umber to darken part of the area under the flowers.

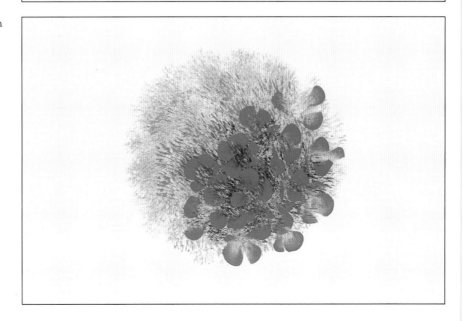

3 Side load a ¼-inch (6mm) angle brush with Dark Blue and paint rose petal strokes (see page 16) to fill in part of the flower ball.

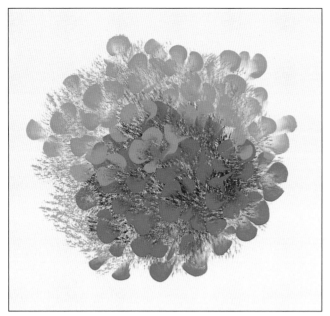

4 Paint rose petal strokes with a ¼-inch (6mm) angle brush side loaded with Medium Blue. Overlap part of the Dark Blue strokes done in the previous step.

5 Fill in the rest of the flower area with petal strokes of Medium Mauve plus a small amount of Dark Blue, side loaded with a ¼-inch (6mm) angle brush.

6 Add overlapping petal strokes in the mauve section with Light Mauve and the Dark Mauve mix plus a small amount of Dark Blue.

7 Create a light blue section by painting petal strokes with Light Blue. Reinforce these strokes with side loads of Sky Blue Pearl. Place some dots in the centers of a few of the flowers with Light Blue. Paint stem lines with the Dark Green mix.

ROSES

Palette

- Very Light Mauve
- Light Mauve
- Medium Mauve
- Dark Mauve mix
- White Pearl
- Buttermilk

1 Basecoat the roses with Medium Mauve. Transfer the rest of the pattern lines with white graphite. Shade the throat and base of the roses with a 1-inch (25mm) flat brush side loaded with the Dark Mauve mix. Use a no. 10 flat brush side loaded with this same mix to shade the small triangle sections on either side of the rose throats.

2 Double load a ½-inch (13mm) angle brush with Light Mauve on the long half of the brush and the Dark Mauve mix on the short half of the brush. Paint the two bottom petal strokes with the Light Mauve toward the outside.

3 With the same double-loaded brush used in step 2, paint the next two overlapping strokes.

4 With the same double-loaded brush used in step 3, paint the next two overlapping strokes.

5 With the same double-loaded brush used in step 4, paint two additional petal strokes that will stay to the inside of the petals painted in step 4.

6 Highlight the outside edges of the remaining petals with a no. 8 flat side loaded with Light Mauve.

7 Reinforce the highlighting on all but the lowest petals with a no. 6 flat side loaded with Very Light Mauve.

8 Reinforce the highlighting on the upper petals with a no. 4 flat side loaded with White Pearl. Side load the dark petal tips with the Dark Mauve mix on a no. 4 flat. Lightly stipple the flower centers in with a no. 0 round loaded with Buttermilk.

ROSEBUDS

Palette

- Very Light Mauve
- Light Mauve
- Medium Mauve
- Dark Mauve mix
- White Pearl
- Light Green mix
- Dark Green mix

1 Basecoat the buds with Medium Mauve. Side load a no. 14 flat with the Dark Mauve mix and shade the bases and throats of the buds.

2 Highlight the buds with a no. 12 flat side loaded with Light Mauve.

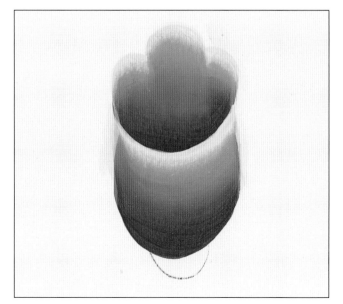

3 Reinforce the highlights with a no. 10 flat side loaded with Very Light Mauve.

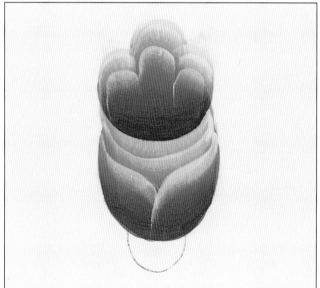

4 Create the inner petals with a no. 8 flat side loaded with Very Light Mauve.

5 Paint the outer petals with a ⅜-inch (10mm) angle brush double loaded with Very Light Mauve and the Dark Mauve mix. The Very Light Mauve should be on the long half of the brush and the Dark Mauve mix on the shorter half of the brush. The Very Light Mauve should face the outer edges of the petals.

6 Reinforce the highlights with a no. 6 flat side loaded with White Pearl. Create the dark petal edges with a no. 4 flat side loaded with the Dark Mauve mix.

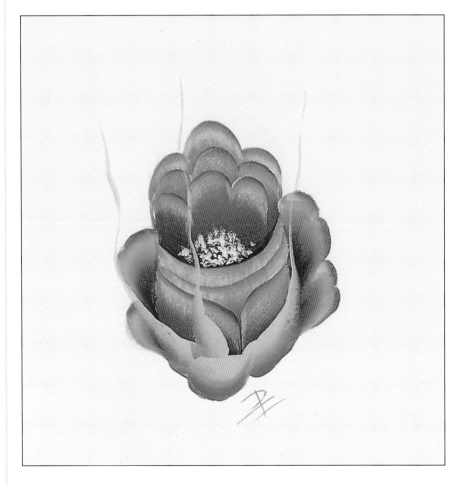

7 Double load a no. 4 filbert with the Light Green mix and the Dark Green mix and use this to paint the calyxes on the buds.

Detail of tray

This pattern may be hand-traced or photocopied for personal use only. Enlarge both sides of the pattern at 145% to return the image to full size. Line up along dotted lines.

Advanced Stroke Roses: Mauve Rose Tray

White Currants and Roses

This lovely punched tin piece is the perfect container for fragrant potpourri—a rose-scented potpourri would be particularly appropriate. The punched tin allows the subtle fragrance to waft into your home.

I had a wonderful time designing and painting this piece. I'd wanted to include white currants in a painting for a long time but had never gotten around to it. These glowing fruits are translucent—if you look closely you can see the seeds in the centers. It was a fun challenge to capture the light that glows through the currants.

The many-petaled roses are a lot easier to paint than you might imagine. An intermediate painter can have great success with this project. I spent several days looking for a way to paint a realistic rose that wasn't too difficult. You begin by loosely filling in the colors and shading in the centers of the flowers. After this step, all that remains is to side load the highlights and the blush on the petal edges! It looks a lot more difficult than it is.

If you're looking for a smaller pattern, the large center rose with its surrounding leaves would lend itself to many smaller pieces. For a really dramatic piece, paint this design on a Black Green background. I know you'll really enjoy painting this project. It works up quickly with beautiful results.

Materials

Palette
DecoArt Americana acrylic paints
- Antique Gold Deep
- Antique Maroon
- Asphaltum
- Eggshell
- Graphite
- Hauser Dark Green
- Jade Green
- Light Avocado
- Midnite Green
- Mississippi Mud
- Olde Gold
- Plantation Pine
- Sand
- Shale Green
- Slate Grey
- Titanium (Snow) White

Surface
This punched tin container with wooden lid can be purchased from Covered Bridge Crafts, 449 Amherst Street, Nashua, NH 03063. (800) 405-4464.

Brushes
To paint this project, you will need a Loew-Cornell series 7600, ¾-inch (19mm) filbert mop for painting the background, no. 4 through no. 14 flats, a no. 00 script liner, no. 6 and no. 8 filberts, a small round or liner, and a Winsor & Newton series 12, no. 4.

Miscellaneous
You will need an old toothbrush for spattering the background.

Preparation

Seal and sand both sides of the wooden lid, then basecoat the lid with Slate Grey. After the paint is thoroughly dry, basecoat the top of the lid again with Slate Grey, this time thinned with a small amount of water. While the Slate Grey is still wet, pick up some Graphite with your ¾-inch (19mm) filbert mop brush. Blend the Graphite into the wet Slate Grey basecoat with slip-slap motions of the brush, working from the lower right toward the upper left. You will need to repeat this step several times to get the Graphite dark enough. You're looking for an even transition in value from the Slate Grey to the Graphite—each time you reload the brush, start blending again from the lower right toward the upper left. Leave some brush marks showing—they add character and interest

to the background.

After the background is thoroughly dry, spatter the top of the lid with Shale Green thinned with water, as illustrated on page 125. Make sure to practice this on a piece of scrap paper before you spatter on your blended lid. If there is too much water in the paint, it will create large drips, and if there is too little water, the paint will stick to the toothbrush. When the spattering is thoroughly dry, you can transfer the pattern.

Painting Procedure

The best way to paint this piece is to work from the bottom up. Start with the white currants, then paint the rose under the leaves, the leaves, and finally the large center rose.

Rosebud

The rosebud on the left side can be painted at any time. Paint the bud using the same progression as the larger roses. Basecoat the calyx with Light Avocado, then highlight it with side loads of Jade Green. Side load the shading with Plantation Pine and add accents of Antique Maroon.

Leaves

In this design you will be working with warm and cool green leaves, which add additional visual interest. The cooler leaves recede and the warmer leaves come forward. The warm leaves are indicated with a "W" on the pattern on page 106 and the cool leaves with a "C."

CURRANTS

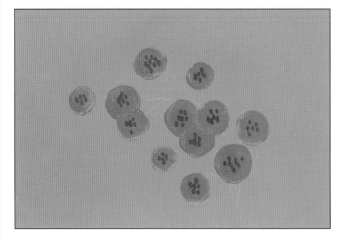

1 Basecoat the currants with Antique Gold Deep. Make a mix of 2 parts Light Avocado + 1 part Antique Gold Deep + 1 part Antique Maroon. Thin this mix with a little water and use a no. 4 liner or any small round brush to paint the seeds in the centers of the currants.

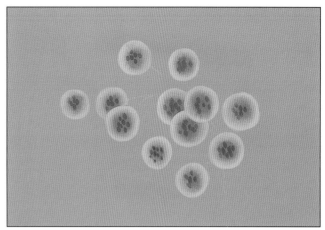

2 Side load a no. 6 flat with Jade Green and float this color completely around the currants. The best way to accomplish this is to float several C-strokes (see page 18) around the outside edges of the currants, overlapping the strokes until you have established the color all the way around the outside edges.

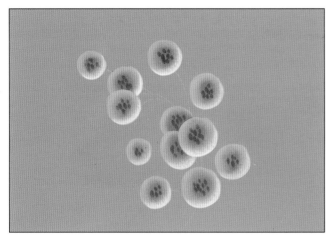

3 Side load a no. 4 flat with Sand and paint C-strokes on the lower right sides of the currants.

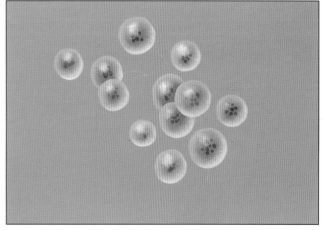

4 Side load a no. 6 flat or filbert with Sand and paint a bull's-eye side load on the upper left of the currants (see page 15).

5 Using the tip of a small round or liner, dab in Mississippi Mud to form the blossom ends of the currants. Dab Asphaltum around the outsides of the blossom ends and place a dot in the center of each. Paint the detail lines with a script liner and thinned Sand. Place high shines on the currants with dots of Titanium White. Basecoat all the stems with Light Avocado using a liner brush. Shade the stems with lines of Plantation Pine.

Palette
- Antique Gold Deep
- Light Avocado
- Antique Maroon
- Jade Green
- Sand
- Mississippi Mud
- Asphaltum
- Titanium White
- Plantation Pine

LEAVES

1 Steps 1 and 2 for the leaves are painted using a wet-on-wet technique. All of the basecoating and blending should be accomplished while the paint is still wet. Work only one leaf at a time. Using a no. 8 filbert, loosely basecoat the light value area of the warm leaf with Light Avocado. Next, basecoat the shadow area with Plantation Pine and loosely blend the two areas of color. Now, roughly blend some Olde Gold into the light value area. It's OK for brush marks to show. Paint the cool leaves in the same manner but brush mix some Hauser Dark Green into the Light Avocado and Plantation Pine to cool the colors.

Palette
- Light Avocado
- Plantation Pine
- Olde Gold
- Hauser Dark Green
- Antique Maroon
- Midnite Green
- Jade Green
- Slate Grey

2 While step 1 is still wet, blend some Antique Maroon into the shadow side of the leaf.

3 Use a no. 12 flat side loaded with Plantation Pine to shade one outside edge, the bases and both sides of the center veins on the warm green leaves. Shade the cool green leaves as shown above using Hauser Dark Green plus a small amount of Plantation Pine. Reinforce the shading in the darkest value areas with Midnite Green.

4 Paint the vein lines with a script liner using Light Avocado for the warm leaves and Light Avocado plus a small amount of Hauser Dark Green for the cool leaves. Side load a no. 6 flat with Light Avocado and highlight one side of the side veins on the warm green leaves. Cool this color with Hauser Dark Green and highlight the side veins on the cool green leaves.

5 Reinforce the highlight edge of the leaves and a few of the side veins with side loads of Jade Green on the warm green leaves. Use Jade Green plus a small amount of Hauser Dark Green on the cool green leaves. Paint a reflected shine on a few of the leaves with side loads of Slate Grey. Where the shine occurs away from the edges of the leaves, use a back-to-back side load as described on page 15. Side load a no. 4 flat with Antique Maroon and accent some of the edges and tips of the leaves.

ROSES

Palette

- Antique Gold Deep
- Olde Gold
- Light Avocado
- Antique Maroon
- Shale Green
- Eggshell
- Titanium White

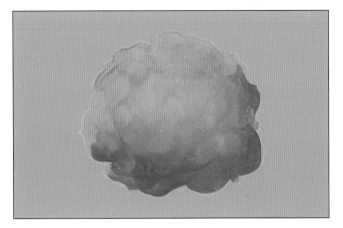

1 All of step 1 should be completed on one rose while the paint is still wet so you can blend between the colors. Using a no. 8 filbert, loosely basecoat the upper section of the first rose shape with Antique Gold Deep. Fill in the center area with Olde Gold and blend between the areas. Make a mix of 2 parts Light Avocado + 1 part Antique Gold Deep + 1 part Antique Maroon. Use this color to basecoat the bottom and right edge, then roughly blend it into the other colors.

2 Transfer the pattern lines for the individual rose petals using white graphite. Side load a no. 12 flat with Shale Green and highlight the petal edges on the upper portion of the rose. Use a no. 14 flat on the larger petals on the lower portion of the rose. Start each highlight with the chisel edge of the brush against the edge of the petal. If you are a light-handed painter, you may need to repeat this step.

3 Side load a no. 10 flat with Eggshell and reinforce all the highlighting on the upper portion of the rose. Use a no. 12 for the lower, larger petals.

4 Side load a no. 8 flat with Titanium White and reinforce all the highlighting on the rose petals. Continue to side load Titanium White on the petals on the upper left side of the rose until they are noticeably lighter than the petals on the lower right.

5 Side load a no. 8 flat with thinned Antique Maroon and float a blush on the outsides of the petals. Concentrate on the pointed parts of the petal edges. Make some darker than others and leave some Titanium White. Stipple Olde Gold plus Titanium White in the center of the largest rose.

Pattern for lid

This pattern may be hand-traced or photocopied for personal use only.

Finishing

When you have finished your painting, you can varnish the lid with the acrylic varnish of your choice, fill the tin with potpourri and enjoy your handiwork!

Detail of lid

Clematis With Yellow Roses

One of my greatest joys in life is spending time tending my perennial gardens. I am always amazed that these beautiful blossoms can renew themselves each year. They begin growing every spring from the thawing earth and come to life as the days lengthen and the temperatures climb. I can't remember a time in my life that I didn't love flowers of all types. My gardens create a treasured, serene haven from the everyday stresses of life. If I find myself worried or distracted by problems, I can take a short walk among the flowers and find some calm space and a new focus.

I also enjoy photographing my flowers and gardens. During our bleak New England winters, the photos are a wonderful reminder that spring and summer will come again. I keep my flower photos in several albums to use for reference material for my paintings. It is such a delight to use pigments to capture the fleeting beauty of these blossoms that I've nurtured in my gardens. It is an even greater pleasure to be able to share my flowers with all my painting friends.

The clematis blossoms on this piece were photographed three years ago. I love these extravagant flowering vines, but have always had limited success growing them. After years of struggling with this vine, it finally burst into glorious bloom—a long-awaited success! I am so glad I photographed it then, because it has never been as pretty since.

I have included the photographs I used to create this painting with this chapter. The yellows create a lovely complement to the violet clematis blossoms. It was a happy discovery to find that the pink tones on these yellow roses coordinate with the pinks in the center vein areas of the clematis blossoms. Carrying these same colors on both flower forms helps to create harmony in the design. I used more pink on the clematis in the painting than you see in the photograph. This also helps to coordinate the two flowers. It is a challenge to design a harmonious painting from a group of separate pictures, so finding a color common to both flowers is a gift of sorts. By including the same pinks as accent tones on the leaves, the entire painting becomes a coherent visual image.

This is an elegant, dressy piece that will be treasured for years to come. It is a fun challenge for the advanced acrylic painter, but all you need to paint this piece is a strong side-loading technique. If you have developed your painting skills by progressing through the pieces in this book, you should have the expertise to paint this piece. Don't be afraid to try it because it looks difficult. Just remember that you can "eat an elephant if you do it one bite at a time." You can paint this piece in the same manner—one flower petal and one leaf at a time. Most of all, enjoy the process. Working on the painting can be more fun than admiring the finished piece.

Materials

Palette
- Antique Maroon
- Black Green
- Burgundy Wine
- Cranberry Wine
- Dove Grey
- French Grey Blue
- Golden Straw
- Jade Green
- Light Avocado
- Light Buttermilk
- Neutral Grey
- Pineapple
- Plantation Pine
- Primary Red
- Primary Yellow
- Raw Umber
- Reindeer Moss Green
- Royal Purple
- Spice Pink
- Summer Lilac
- Taupe
- Titanium (Snow) White

Surface
This lovely, ball-footed jewelry box can be purchased from Covered Bridge Crafts, 449 Amherst Street, Nashua, NH 03063. (800) 405-4464.

Brushes
To paint this project, you will need a large flat for basecoating the piece, a Loew-Cornell series 7600, ¾-inch (19mm) filbert mop to create the blended background, no. 6 through no. 14 flats, a ¾-inch (19mm) flat, a no. 0 round, no. 6 through no. 10 filberts and a good script liner.

Miscellaneous
A candle and an old knife for the smoking on the sides. Gold leaf and leaf adhesive for leafing the lid and the feet.

I loved the color of this rose but felt the complexity of the petal arrangement would not be a good choice for this painting, so I used the color but not the shape.

I used the shapes of the large pink rose at left and the smaller, less opened one at right to create this painting.

Here are photos of the clematis bud and one of the flowers I used to create this painting.

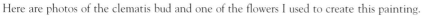

Preparation

Seal and sand the box inside and out. Basecoat the top of the lid and the sides of the box with Dove Grey. When the lid is dry, dampen the surface with clean water and then basecoat the top of the lid again with Dove Grey thinned with water. Quickly pick up Raw Umber with the ¾-inch (19mm) filbert mop and blend this color into the wet background, starting from the lower left corner and working toward the upper right. Use a slip-slap motion of the brush to blend the colors together. You will need to reinforce the Raw Umber a couple of times. When you have worked in enough Raw Umber, wipe the brush and pick up Light Buttermilk and begin blending this from the upper right toward the lower left. Again, you will need to reinforce this a couple of times. Next, pick up Taupe and blend this color randomly into the background. Let the surface dry.

Make a thin side load of Dark Green (Plantation Pine) on a ¾-inch (19mm) flat and float some green into the background. When dry, transfer the pattern. Float more thinned Dark Green (Plantation Pine) behind the small rose and a few of the other design elements.

Painting Procedure

Set up your palette as described on page 13 with the value scales on the next page. The individual palettes and step-by-step instructions will use the value names listed in the left column, rather than the bottle names or mixes.

Paint the leaves first, the clematis second and the roses last. You need not bring all the highlights, accents and shadows to their final stage until you've completed the basic form of the design elements.

I created a focal area where the large, fully opened rose meets the clematis blossoms. All the lightest value highlights and the strongest contrasts in value and between complementary colors are in this area. After all the design elements are completed, you can balance the painting by carrying your palette colors throughout your design. For example, you will find yellow, violet and pink accents on the leaves, helping them to harmonize with the flowers. There are also yellow accents on the lavender clematis and a few lavender accents on the roses. Be very careful not to make these lavender accents on the roses too strong or numerous, or the rose will begin to vibrate with the strong contrast in complementary colors.

Leaves

Complete the leaves except for the last step. It's best not to paint the accents until the flowers are finished, because it's difficult to know how much of an accent you'll need in any area until the roses and clematis are painted. Here are a few thoughts that may help you with placing accents: They should be painted where they will help to harmonize the painting. Remember to keep the accents in areas of similar value. For example, if you are painting a deep maroon accent (a very dark value), you should place it in a shadow area of the leaf. If you painted it in a highlight area, there would be too much contrast between the highlight and the accent, and it would probably be distracting in the design. Look for areas where a color would logically be reflected onto the leaves, such as the lavender accents on the two leaves on the upper right of the design. By reflecting the clematis colors onto the leaves, it helps the leaves harmonize with the flowers.

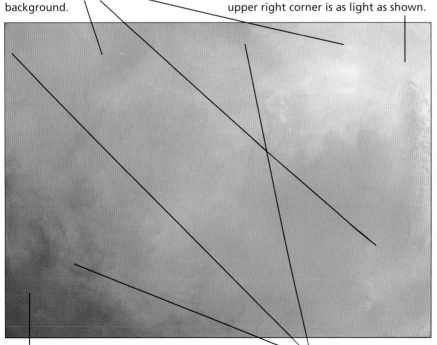

Blend Taupe randomly into the wet background.

Reinforce the Light Buttermilk until the upper right corner is as light as shown.

Reinforce the Raw Umber until the lower left corner is as dark as shown.

After the background is dry, float a few thin washes of Dark Green.

VERY LIGHT GREEN	Reindeer Moss Green
LIGHT GREEN	Jade Green
MEDIUM GREEN	Light Avocado
DARK GREEN	Plantation Pine
VERY DARK GREEN	2 parts Plantation Pine + 1 part Black Green
VERY LIGHT VIOLET	2 parts Titanium White + 1 part Summer Lilac
LIGHT VIOLET	1 part Titanium White + 1 part Summer Lilac
MEDIUM VIOLET	Summer Lilac
DARK VIOLET	1 part Summer Lilac + 1 part Royal Purple
VERY DARK VIOLET	Royal Purple
VERY LIGHT PINK	2 part Titanium White + 1 part Spice Pink
LIGHT PINK	Spice Pink
MEDIUM PINK	1 part Burgundy Wine + 1 part Cranberry Wine + ½ part Golden Straw
DARK PINK	1 part Cranberry Wine + 1 part Antique Maroon
VERY DARK PINK	Antique Maroon
LIGHT YELLOW	Pineapple
MEDIUM YELLOW	Golden Straw
MEDIUM ORANGE	3 parts Primary Yellow + 1 part Primary Red
DARK ORANGE	2 parts Medium Orange mix + 1 part Antique Maroon

Clematis

Next paint the clematis blossoms and bud. Try to keep the lightest value areas and areas of greatest contrast in the focal area at the upper right of the large rose. Notice how the left petals on the upper left clematis blossom seem to fade into the background. I made a thin wash of Medium Yellow and Neutral Grey and washed this over the flower petals. This toned yellow wash neutralizes the intensity of the lavender flower petals as well as reduces the contrast in values. It also helps to create lost edges between the petals and the background. All of this helps to keep these petals from leading the eye out of the painting and distracting from the focal area. Be very careful if you choose to use this wash, however, as it is very easy to turn the lavender petals muddy if you apply too heavy a wash. As with the leaves, you do not have to finalize all the accents until all the design elements are painted. It is also a good idea not to bring all the highlights to their lightest value until you have the roses painted.

Roses

The large rose has the strongest accents, lightest value highlights and darkest shadows. Be careful when placing very dark shadows on roses—always remember that flowers are translucent. The shadows will never be as dark as they would be on a solid object. Avoid outlining each petal with a dark value, as this will give you the look of plastic flowers. If you remember to keep some lost edges in the

roses and carefully control the dark values, you will create realistic, soft-looking flowers. Paint the smaller rose on the right with less contrast in value than the large rose. If you get the smaller rose too light in value with too much contrast, it will distract from the focal area and lead the eye out of the painting.

Stems

The stem for the small rose is base-coated with Medium Green, then highlighted and shaded with the rest of the green value scale. The thorns are painted with Medium Pink and then shaded with Very Dark Pink. The highlights on the thorns are the base-coat plus some Light Buttermilk. The cut end of the stem is basecoated with Very Light Green and then shaded with Medium Green. The stem for the clematis bud is basecoated with Medium Green and then shaded with Medium Pink, then Dark Pink.

Accents and Cast Shadows

Once you have finished the basic painting on all the design elements, you can add or adjust the accents on the leaves and clematis. Remember that accents should enhance and harmonize the design elements. They should not be "screaming" for attention. This is also a good time to paint the cast shadows on the leaves and clematis. To create the cast shadows from the rose stem on the clematis petals, make a wash of Very Dark Violet and paint this thinned purple following the shape of the flower petals. The cast shadows on the leaves are painted with a wash of the Very Dark Green mix. Just remember when painting shadows—the shape of the shadows reflects the shape of the object casting the shadow *and* the shape of the object the shadow is falling on.

(Continued on page 121.)

LEAVES

1 Basecoat the leaves with Medium Green. Side load highlights with Light Green and then reinforce them in the lightest value areas with Very Light Green.

2 Shade the leaves with side loads of Dark Green. Reinforce the shadows with side loads of the Very Dark Green mix in the darkest value areas.

3 Make a mix of Medium Green plus a small amount of Light Green and paint the veins.

4 Shade under the side veins with side loads of Dark Green. On a few of the leaves, deepen the shadow against the center vein opposite the light source.

5 Pull small feeder veins with a mix of Medium Green plus a small amount of Light Green. Float accents of the Dark Violet mix, the Dark Pink mix and thinned Medium Yellow. Float a few areas of reflected light with French Grey Blue. To create a bug bite, paint the hole in the leaf with whatever color is underneath the leaf. Float around the bug bite with Very Dark Pink and then paint an irregular line of Very Dark Pink on the edge of the bug bite.

Palette
- Very Light Green
- Light Green
- Medium Green
- Dark Green
- Very Dark Green mix
- Dark Violet mix
- Dark Pink mix
- Very Dark Pink
- Medium Yellow
- French Grey Blue

CLEMATIS

1 Basecoat the flower with Medium Violet. Tint the center vein areas of the flower petals with side loads of Burgundy Wine.

2 Highlight between the center veins with side loads of Medium Violet. Reinforce the lightest of these with Light Violet mix. Create the rest of the highlights with side loads of Light Violet mix. In the lightest value areas use Very Light Violet mix.

3 Shade with side loads of the Dark Violet mix, then Very Dark Violet in the darkest value areas.

4 Pull vein lines with thinned Dark Violet mix. Highlight between the vein lines in a few areas with thinned Light Violet mix. In a few of the lightest value areas, reinforce the highlights between the veins with thinned Light Buttermilk.

5 Side load accents of Medium Yellow and reflected light with French Grey Blue.

Palette
- Medium Violet
- Burgundy Wine
- Very Light Violet mix
- Light Violet mix
- Dark Violet mix
- Very Dark Violet
- Light Buttermilk
- Medium Yellow
- French Grey Blue

Painting Roses With Deanne Fortnam

CLEMATIS CENTER AND WATER DROPS

Palette
- Very Light Green
- Very Dark Green mix
- Very Dark Pink
- Black Green
- Light Violet mix
- Dark Violet mix
- Titanium White

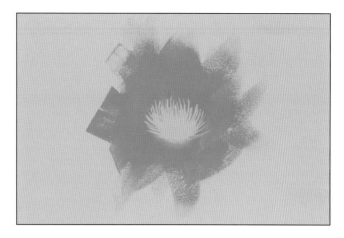

1 Pull lines of Very Light Green with a liner brush to establish the center. Side load Very Light Green against the bottom of the center where it joins the violet part of the clematis.

2 Pull lines of Very Dark Pink from the tips of the stamens toward the center.

3 Darken the tips of the stamens with Very Dark Pink plus some Black Green. Shade against the base of the center with a side load of the Very Dark Green mix. Pull a few short lines of Very Light Green at the bottom of the center.

(2) Shade inside the upper right of the drops with the Dark Violet mix.

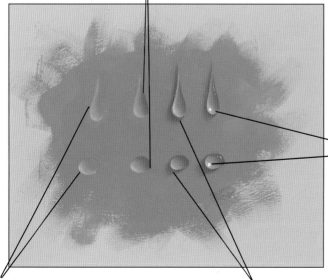

(4) Place high shines of Titanium White with the tip of a liner brush.

(1) Highlight inside the lower left of the drops with the Light Violet mix.

(3) Paint a cast shadow against the lower left of the drops with the Dark Violet mix.

CLEMATIS BUD

Palette
- Very Light Violet mix
- Light Violet mix
- Medium Violet
- Dark Violet mix
- Very Dark Violet
- Medium Pink mix
- Dark Pink mix
- Very Dark Pink
- Dark Green
- Medium Green
- French Grey Blue

1 Basecoat the bud with Medium Violet. Highlight with side loads of the Light Violet mix and then the Very Light Violet mix in the lightest value areas.

2 Paint shadows with side loads of first the Dark Violet mix and then Very Dark Violet.

3 Add side-loaded shadows in the center and on the right and left sides of the bud with a mixture of 2 parts Medium Pink mix + 1 part Dark Pink mix.

4 Side load Dark Green on the tip and the lower right of the bud.

5 Side load a reflected light of French Grey Blue on the lower left of the bud. Paint a dark line of Very Dark Violet plus a small amount of Very Dark Pink in the center of the Very Dark Violet shaded area. Basecoat the stem with Medium Green. Shade with the Medium Pink mix and then reinforce with the Dark Pink mix.

ROSES

1 Basecoat with Medium Yellow. Highlight with side loads of Light Yellow and then reinforce the lightest value areas with Light Yellow plus Light Buttermilk.

2 Side load the shaded sections of the roses with Primary Yellow to intensify the yellow.

Palette
- Light Yellow
- Medium Yellow
- Light Buttermilk
- Primary Yellow
- Medium Orange mix
- Dark Orange mix
- Light Pink
- Medium Pink mix
- Dark Pink mix
- Very Light Green
- Light Green
- Medium Green
- Dark Green
- Very Dark Green mix
- French Grey Blue

3 Shade the roses with side loads of the Medium Orange mix.

4 Reinforce the shading with side loads of the Dark Orange mix. Side load cast shadows under the turned-back edges on the front petals with thinned Dark Orange mix.

5 On the small rose, side load the petal edges with Light Pink. Reinforce the highlighting if necessary. Follow the large rose petal illustrations for the pink application on the large rose.

6 Reinforce the pink tinting on the petal edges with side loads of the Medium Pink mix and then the Dark Pink mix in a few random areas. Don't outline the petals. In a few of the darkest areas, use a liner brush with the Dark Pink mix and darken the tips of the petals. Reinforce the highlighting if necessary. Make a very thin wash of the Medium Orange mix plus the Dark Orange mix and use a very fine liner brush to paint the vein lines. Pull these veins from the base of the petals toward the outer edges. Make a thin wash of Medium Yellow and lighten between the veins in a few areas. Basecoat the calyx with Medium Green. Highlight with side loads of Light Green, then Very Light Green. Shade with side loads of Dark Green, then reinforce with the Very Dark Green mix. Pull vein lines with Dark Green. Pull some fine lines from the tips of the calyxes with the Medium Pink mix plus some Dark Pink mix. Side load some reflected light with French Grey Blue.

LARGE ROSE PETAL

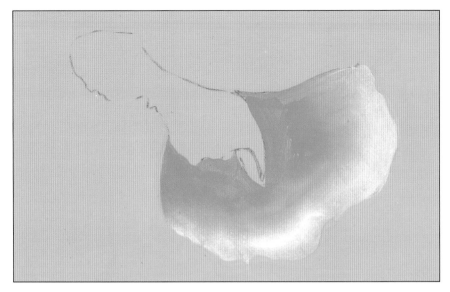

1 Basecoat with Medium Yellow. Highlight with side loads of Light Yellow and then Light Yellow plus Light Buttermilk. In the lightest value areas, highlight with side loads of Light Buttermilk.

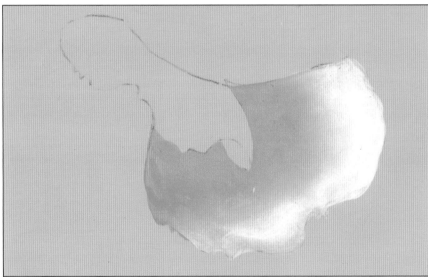

2 Side load Primary Yellow in the shadow areas to intensify the yellow.

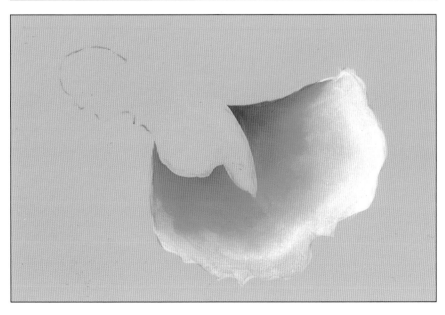

3 Shade with side loads of first the Medium Orange mix and then reinforce with the Dark Orange mix.

Palette

- Light Yellow
- Medium Yellow
- Light Buttermilk
- Primary Yellow
- Medium Orange mix
- Dark Orange mix
- Very Light Pink mix
- Medium Pink mix
- Dark Pink mix
- Very Dark Pink
- French Grey Blue

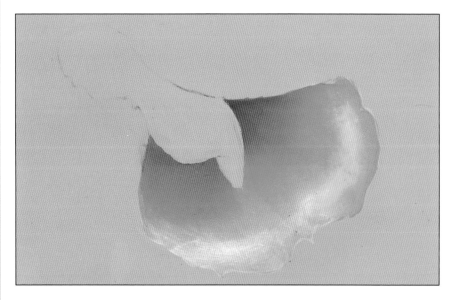

4 Tint the petal edges with side loads of the Very Light Pink mix. Reinforce the highlights.

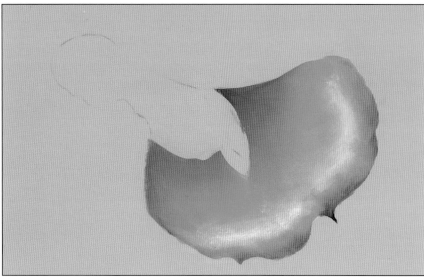

5 Darken some areas of the pink on the petal edges with side loads of the Medium Pink mix. Use a liner to darken the tips of the petal edges with the Very Dark Pink. Reinforce the highlights if necessary.

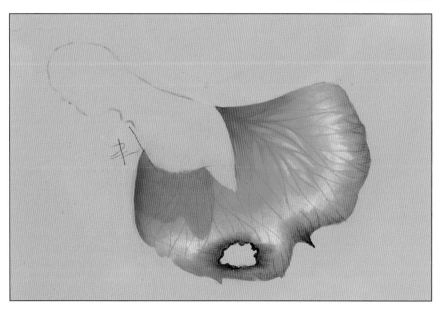

6 Pull vein lines from the base of the petal toward the edge with a mix of thinned Medium Orange mix plus the Dark Orange mix. Pull a few vein lines on the pink edges of the flower petal with thinned Dark Pink mix. Highlight between a few of the veins in the highlight area with thinned Light Buttermilk. Highlight between a few of the veins in the yellow areas with thinned Medium Yellow. Side load reflected light with French Grey Blue. Make a wash of the Dark Orange mix and paint the cast shadow. This must be very washy so all the detailing shows through the shadow. If you wish to create a bug bite in the lower petal, paint the hole with the basecoat color. On the box, I painted the hole with Medium Green, then painted the section of stem and leaf under the hole. Side load around the hole with thinned Very Dark Pink and then paint an irregular line of Very Dark Pink around the edges of the hole.

(Continued from page 112.)

Water Drops

I usually add the water drops last, because I want to see where they can enhance the design without distracting from the focal area. Use the value scale of whatever object you are painting to put in the water drops; for the clematis I used the violet value scale, and for the roses I used the pink value scale. It's usually preferable to place the drops in a medium value area so the highlights and shadows will show to their best advantage. I ordinarily highlight the inside of the drop with the lightest value from whatever value scale the object is painted with, and use the first or second dark value for the shading. I used Light Yellow for the highlights on the drops on the large rose, and the Medium Orange mix plus the Dark Orange mix for the shadows. I placed the high shines with Titanium White on the tip of a liner brush. If I were going to paint drops on the leaves, I would have used Very Light Green for the highlight and the Very Dark Green mix for the shadows. I chose not to paint water drops on the leaves in this design, because they would have led the eye away from the focal area.

Finishing

Work on one side of the box at a time to finish the background and smoking on the bottom of the box. Basecoat again with thinned Dove Grey. Using a ¾-inch (19mm) filbert mop brush, blend Raw Umber, Light Buttermilk and Taupe randomly into the wet Dove Grey. After you have completed the blending and while the paint is still somewhat wet, smoke the sides. This technique gives the box an elegant *faux* finish. After you have completed all four sides of the box, measure ½″ (1.3cm) from the top edge and draw a line around the box. Paint a band of Plantation Pine above the line. Paint the curved, routed edge on the lid with Plantation Pine. Basecoat the ball feet and the edge of the lid with Antique Maroon. Following the instructions on page 126, gold leaf the edge of the lid and the feet. When you have completed all the painting and finishing work, varnish the piece with the acrylic varnish of your choice.

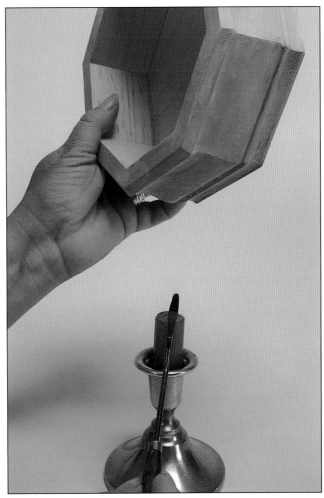

Smoking
Basecoat the area you will be smoking. Hold an old palette knife in the tip of a candle flame until it creates sooty smoke. While the basecoat is still damp (the damp paint will capture the soot), hold the painted surface over the sooty smoke and turn the piece until the desired area has a soft pattern of swirls and veins.

Pattern for the lid.

This pattern may be hand-traced or photocopied for personal use only.

Detail of lid

Detail of smoking and gold leafing

Chapter Four

Finishing Your Projects

After you have taken all the time and trouble to paint the main design on a piece, it's always nice to do something interesting with the rest of the project's surfaces. When I start a painting, I usually don't have any definite ideas of how I'm going to finish embellishing the piece. My ideas usually evolve along with the painting.

I generally start the trims by choosing colors that were used in the main design elements. I often use striping because I love that look.

In project 5 we finished the clock by antiquing, and in project 11 we added a smoked *faux* finish to the box. Some other finishing options are sponging, spattering, stippling, gold leafing and strokework borders, or a combination of several of these techniques. Sometimes when finishing a box where there's room for additional painting, you can repeat an element from the main design, as I did on the sides of the Basic Stroke Rose box on page 32.

Striping

1 Make the pencil point of a compass shorter than the metal point. Place the metal edge of the compass against the edge of the object and pull the pencil along the edge to create a guideline for striping.

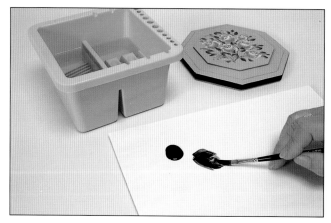

2 Load the dagger brush with paint and dress the paint into the brush by flattening the chisel edge. Flatten the chisel on the opposite side of the brush.

3 Place the chisel edge of the dagger brush against the guideline and pull the line using even pressure on the brush.

Painting Roses With Deanne Fortnam

Sponging

1 Cut a 2″-diameter (5.1cm) circle out of a kitchen sponge. Wet the sponge in clean water and squeeze out the excess water. Pick up some paint on the sponge and smear it across the waxed palette to distribute the paint evenly. Remove the excess.

2 Lightly press the sponge to the surface to create texture, moving the position of the sponge with each tap. Many times I choose several colors from the main design and overlap them to create an interesting finish that coordinates with the design.

Spattering

1 Pick up some water on an old toothbrush. Pick up paint and smear the toothbrush around on your waxed palette to mix the water and paint together.

2 Pull a straightedge palette knife over the bristles so the paint comes off the toothbrush in a spatter pattern.

Stippling

1 Pick up a small amount of paint on the stippling brush. Smear the brush around on the waxed palette to remove excess paint.

2 Lightly tap the brush on the surface to create a light stipple pattern.

Gold Leafing

1 Basecoat the area to be leafed with a maroon or burgundy color. When this is dry, paint the basecoated area with gold leaf adhesive using an old, ruined brush. Don't use a good brush for this step as the leaf adhesive will not come out of the bristles well enough to use the brush for side loading again. Be careful not to get any adhesive on any other part of the painting. The adhesive will appear milky when wet.

2 Pick up a sheet of gold leaf using the tissue paper between the sheets of leaf and lightly crumple the leaf. This will create texture when you apply the gold leaf.

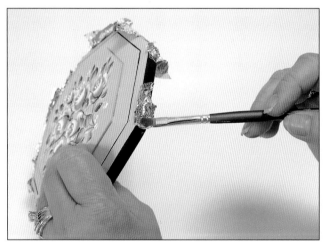

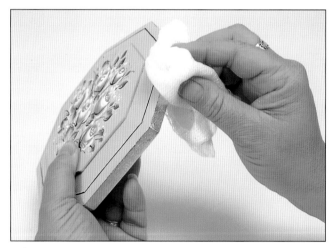

3 When the adhesive is dry and ready for leafing, it will appear clear. Place pieces of gold leaf on the dried adhesive until the area to be leafed is covered.

4 Using a soft pad of cheesecloth or any soft cloth, lightly buff the leafed area to remove any leafing that did not adhere to the adhesive.

Finishing the Interior

Another area not to neglect when finishing a piece is the inside of a box. You can paint it a pretty color as on the Russian box or decorate it with a design. On the Norwegian trunk, I repeated the design from the outside of the trunk on the inside (see page 53). On the Basic Stroke Rose box, I painted a strokework border on the inside of the lid and on the base (see page 32). I have also used a rubber stamp to decorate the inside of a box.

Another lovely way to finish a box is to line it with a pretty fabric. I use cotton prints in colors that coordinate with the colors in the painting. Let your imagination run wild and have fun.

Painting Roses With Deanne Fortnam

Varnishing

The finishing touch for a painted piece is to apply a varnish or finish over the painted surface to protect it. I prefer to use a brush-on varnish and then hand-rub the finish with steel wool to give the piece a lovely, matte, satiny-feeling finish. When you are ready to varnish, make sure to remove all graphite lines from the painting. I use a kneaded eraser for this. You can stop after two coats of varnish, or apply seven coats and create a hand-rubbed finish. A final coat of paste wax will give the piece a glossier finish.

By paying close attention to all the details of a painting, from the proper surface preparation to the final varnishing, you will create heirloom-quality pieces that will remain beautiful for years to come. I hope you will enjoy painting the roses in this book as much as I've enjoyed creating them. Throughout history, roses have been immortalized in literature and art. It's fun to know that by painting these roses, we are part of that tradition.

1 Mix the varnish by rolling the bottle on a tabletop. Shaking the bottle will create bubbles in the varnish. Pick up the varnish with your large one-stroke brush and dress it into the brush on your waxed palette.

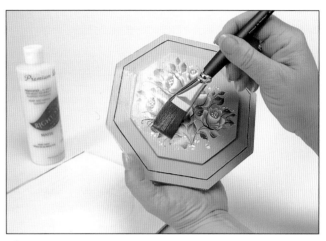

2 Apply a thin, even coat of varnish using long strokes in the direction of the wood grain. Let this dry and then apply another coat, making sure there are no impurities in the first. You can leave the piece with two coats of varnish, or apply four or five more coats and then hand-rub the finish, as described in steps 3 and 4.

3 After applying seven coats of varnish, let the piece cure overnight. Rub the surface of the piece following the direction of the wood grain with 0000 steel wool until you have a smooth, matte finish that is soft to the touch. Pay close attention as you buff the surface: You don't want to wear through the varnish and ruin your painted surface. Wear a dust mask when using steel wool. You can get these at any hardware store. Wipe the piece with a tack cloth.

4 For a glossier finish, apply a coat of paste wax with a piece of cheesecloth. Buff to a satin shine.

Index